# Welcome to 'Enchanted Forests'

Dear Explorer of Wonder,

You hold in your hands a portal to a realm where nature's magic is alive, where every leaf whispers a story, and every color you choose adds to the enchantment. 'Enchanted Forests' is more than just a coloring book; it's a journey through mystical landscapes, a place where imagination takes flight, and serenity becomes your companion.

As you turn these pages, you will wander through magical groves, uncover hidden wonders, and befriend creatures of fantasy and folklore. Each illustration is a lovingly crafted piece of art, waiting for your unique touch to bring it to vibrant life.

We invite you to lose yourself in the intricate details of this enchanted world. Let your creativity flow freely, let your thoughts meander like a tranquil forest stream, and let the colors you choose reflect your innermost feelings and dreams.

Take a deep breath, pick up your colors, and step into the enchanting world of 'Enchanted Forests.' May this journey bring you peace, inspiration, and a renewed sense of wonder.

Happy Coloring!

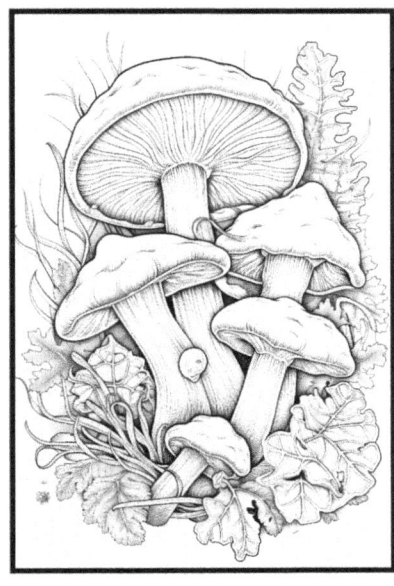
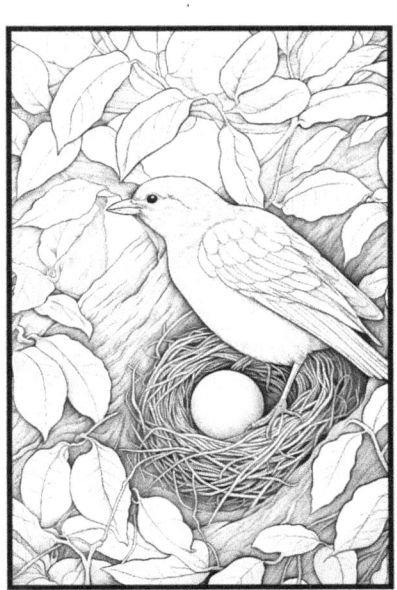
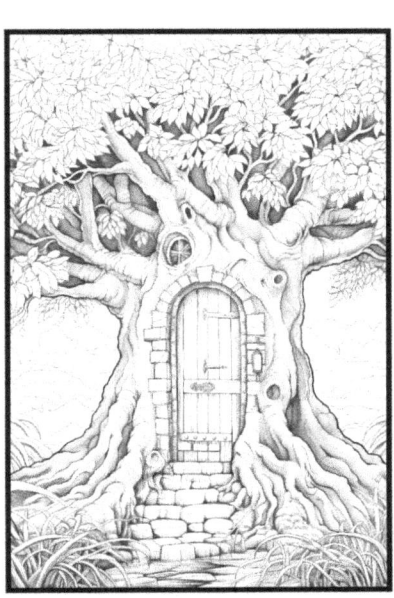

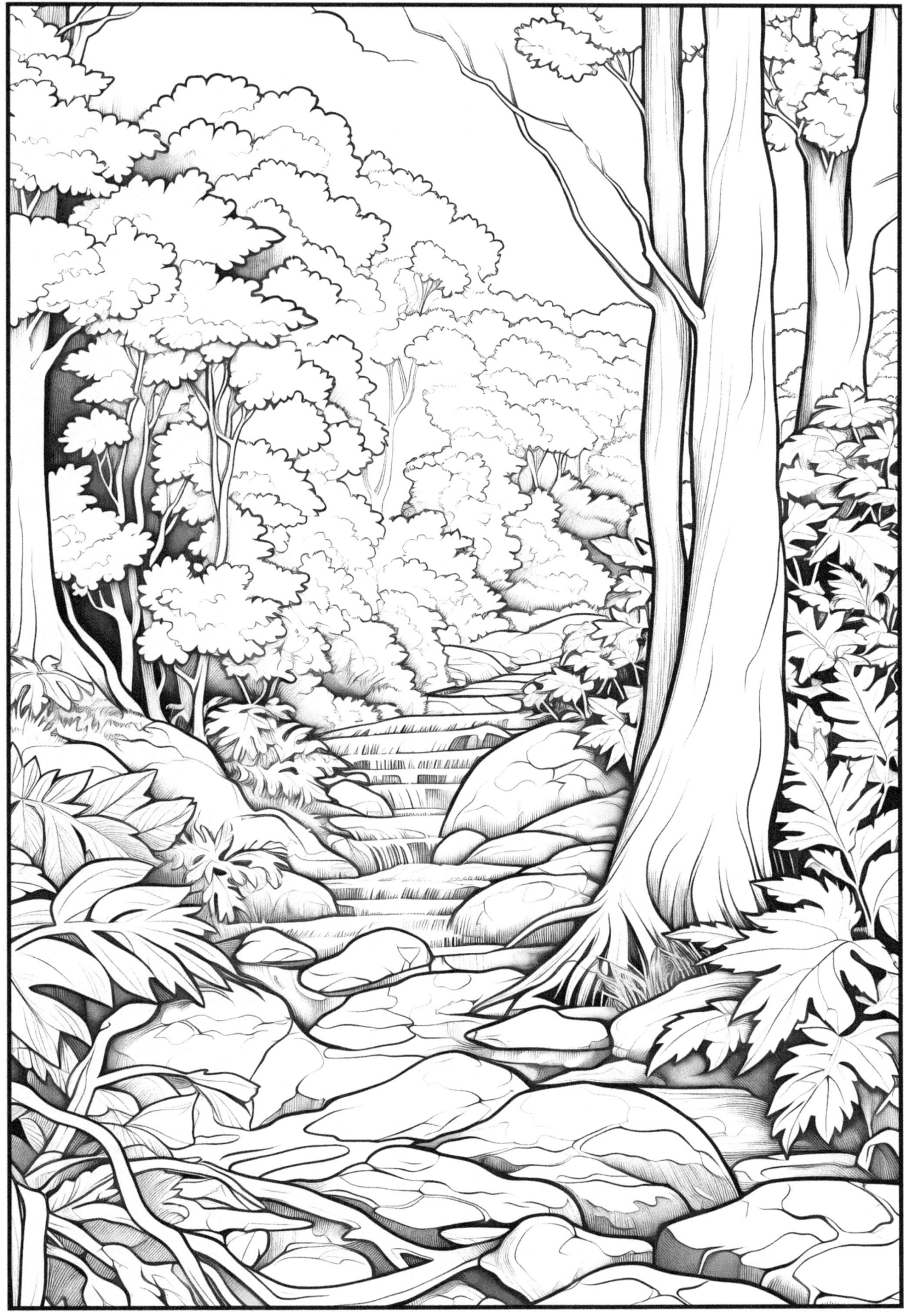

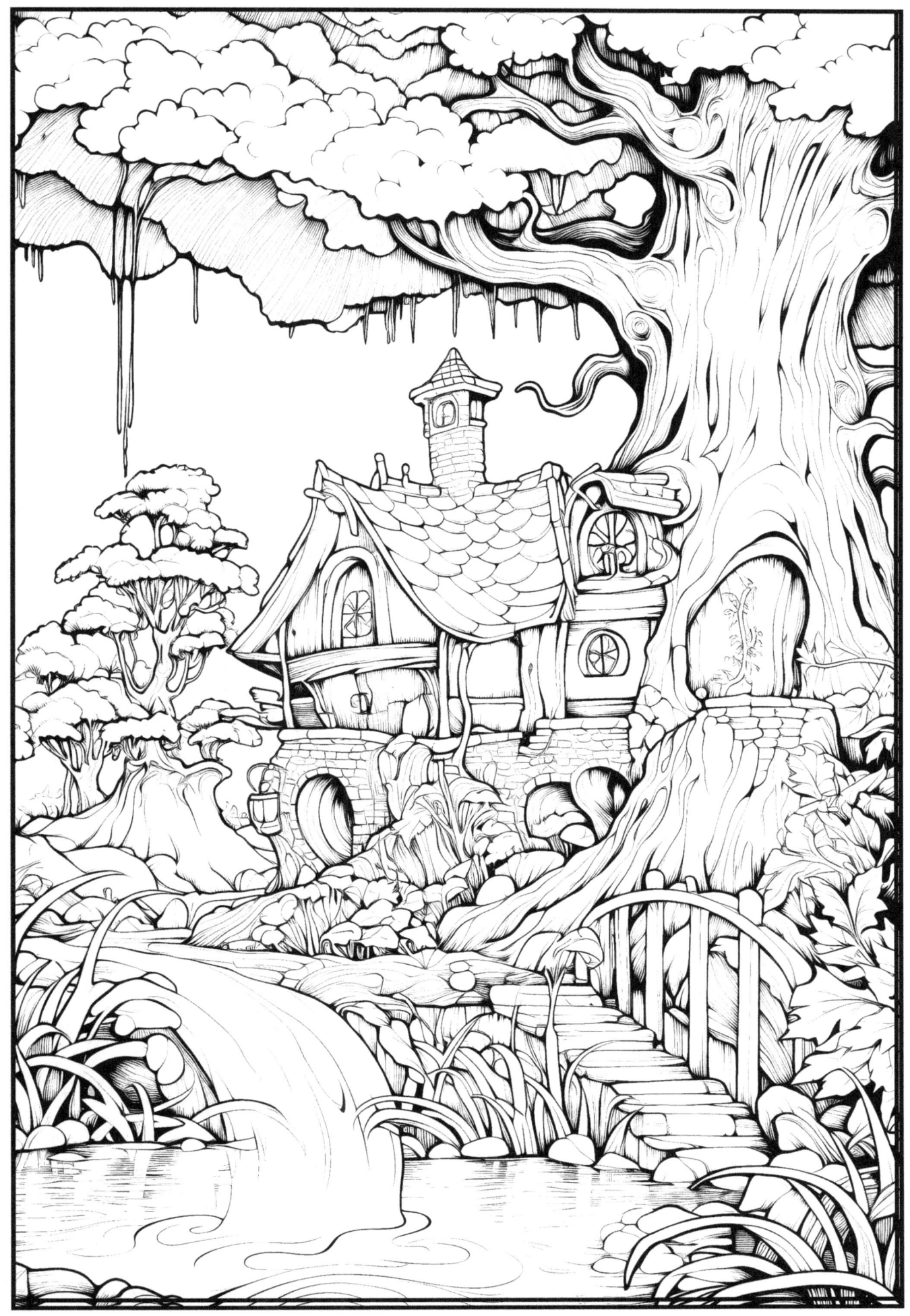

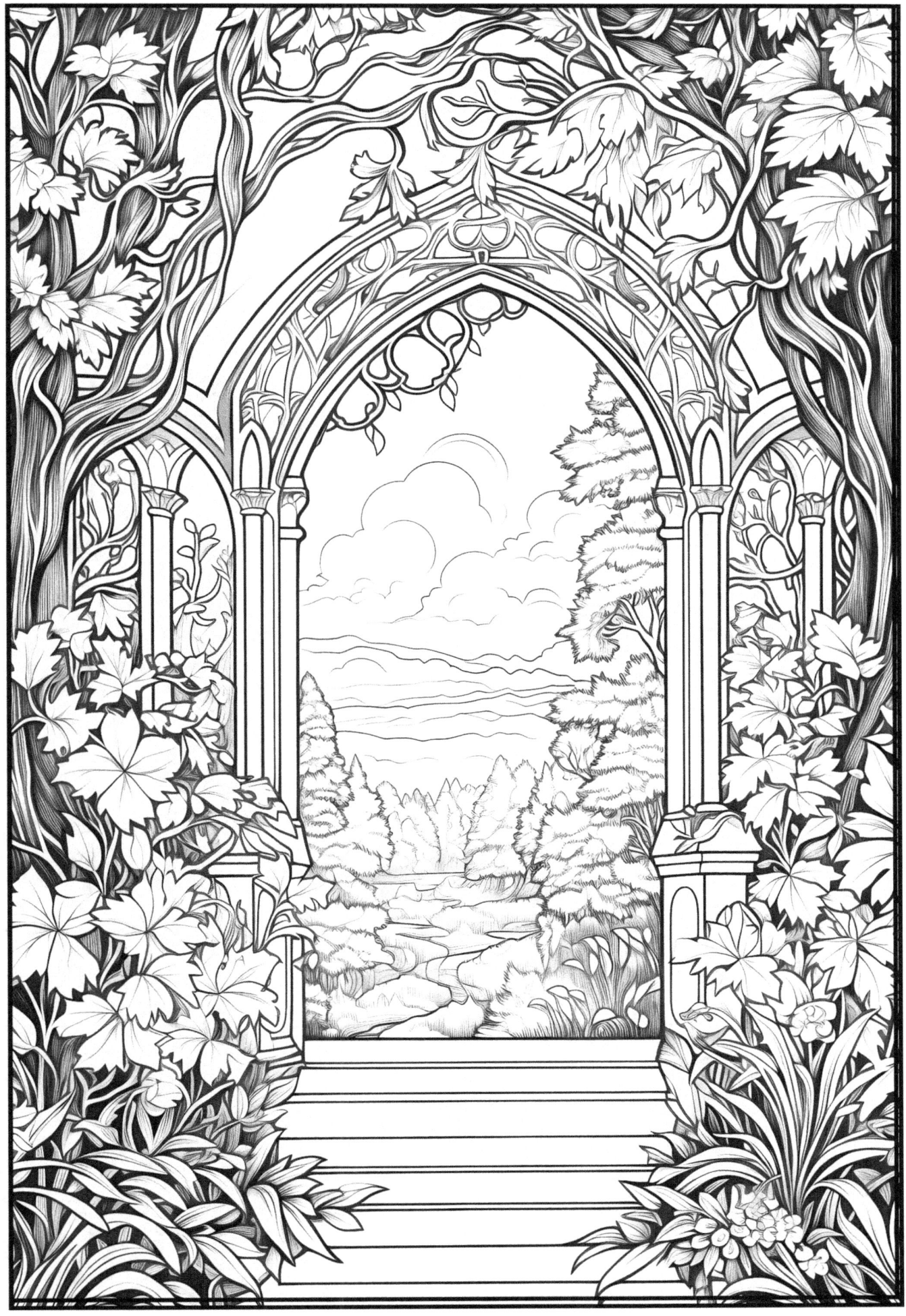

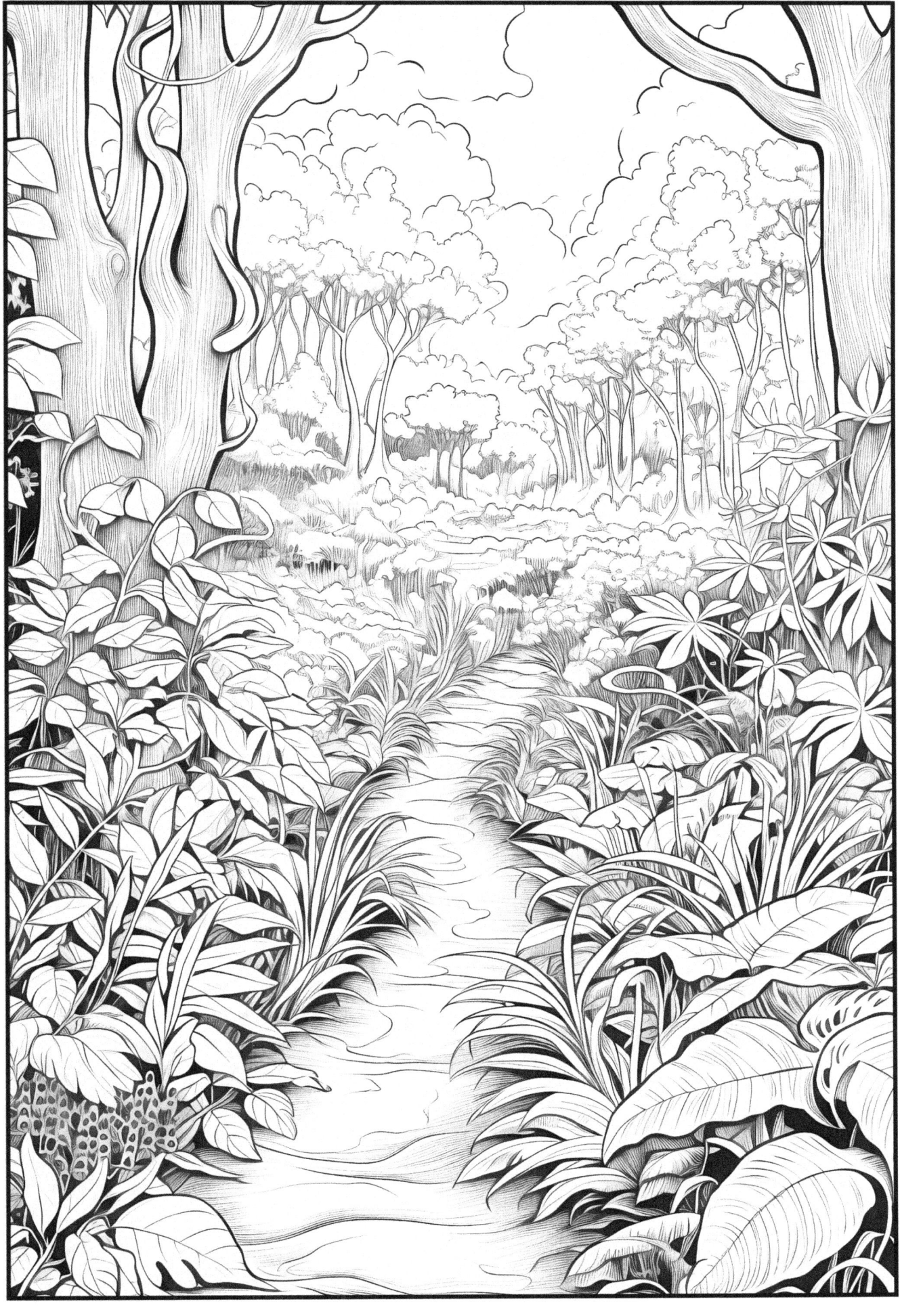

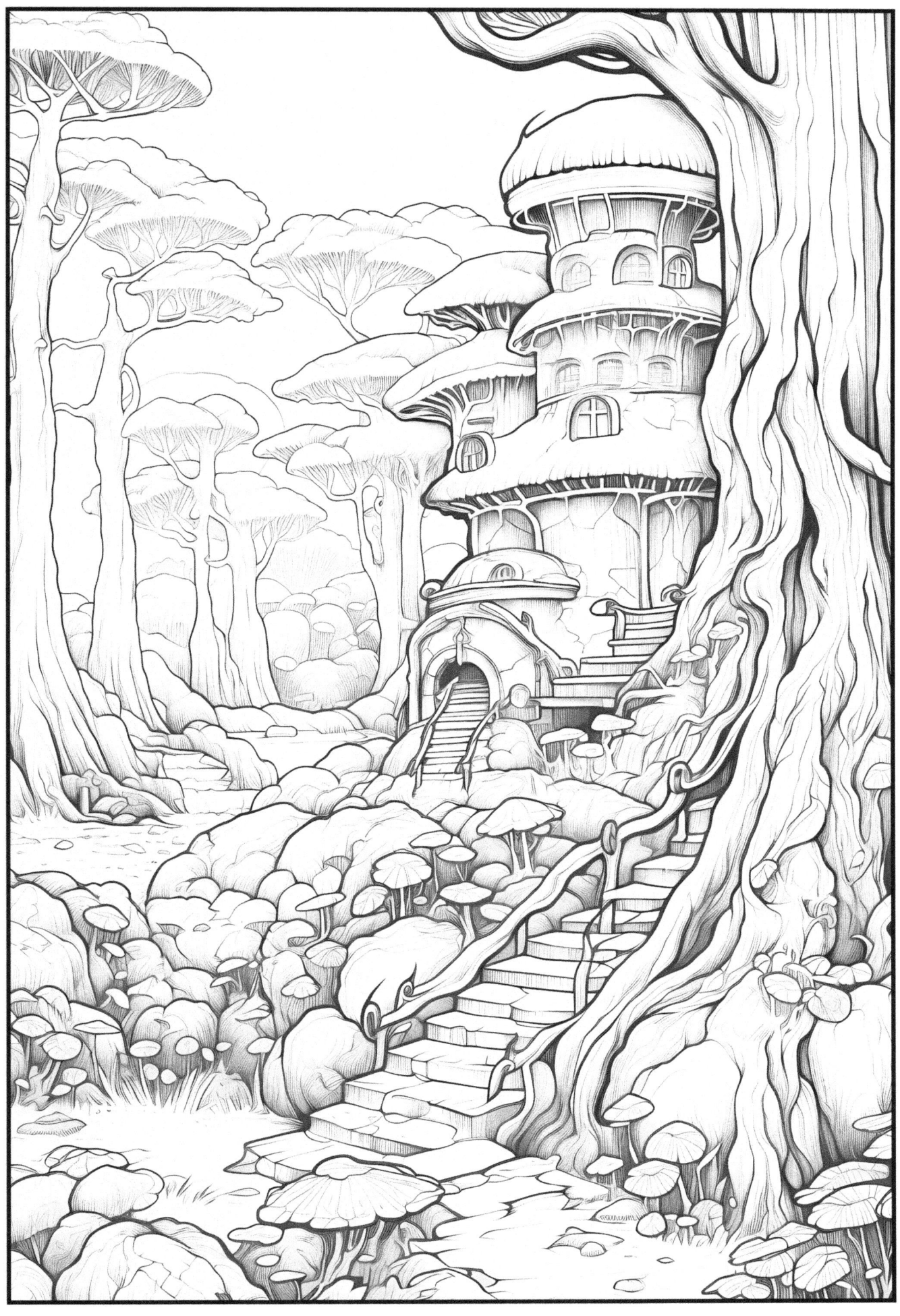

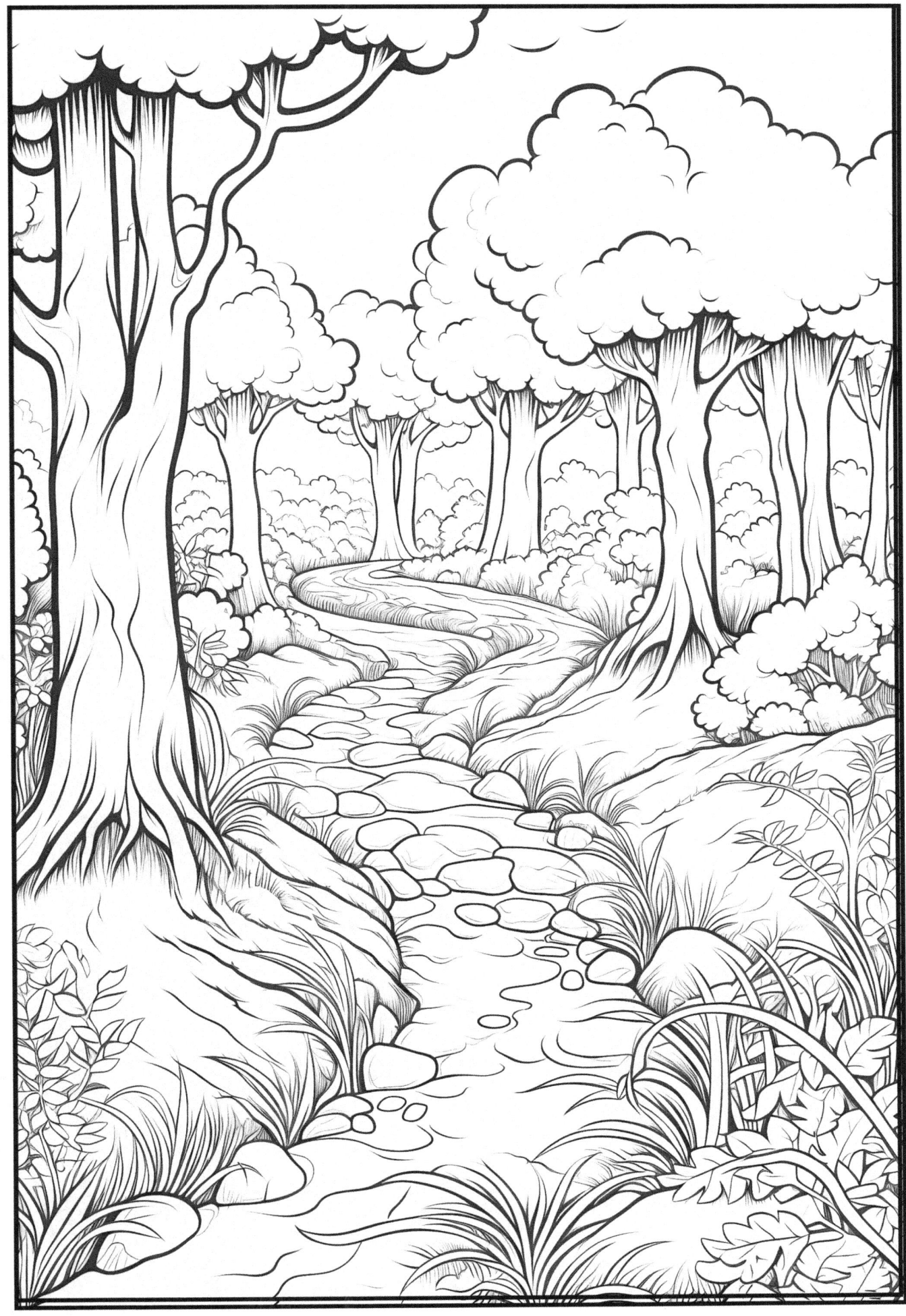

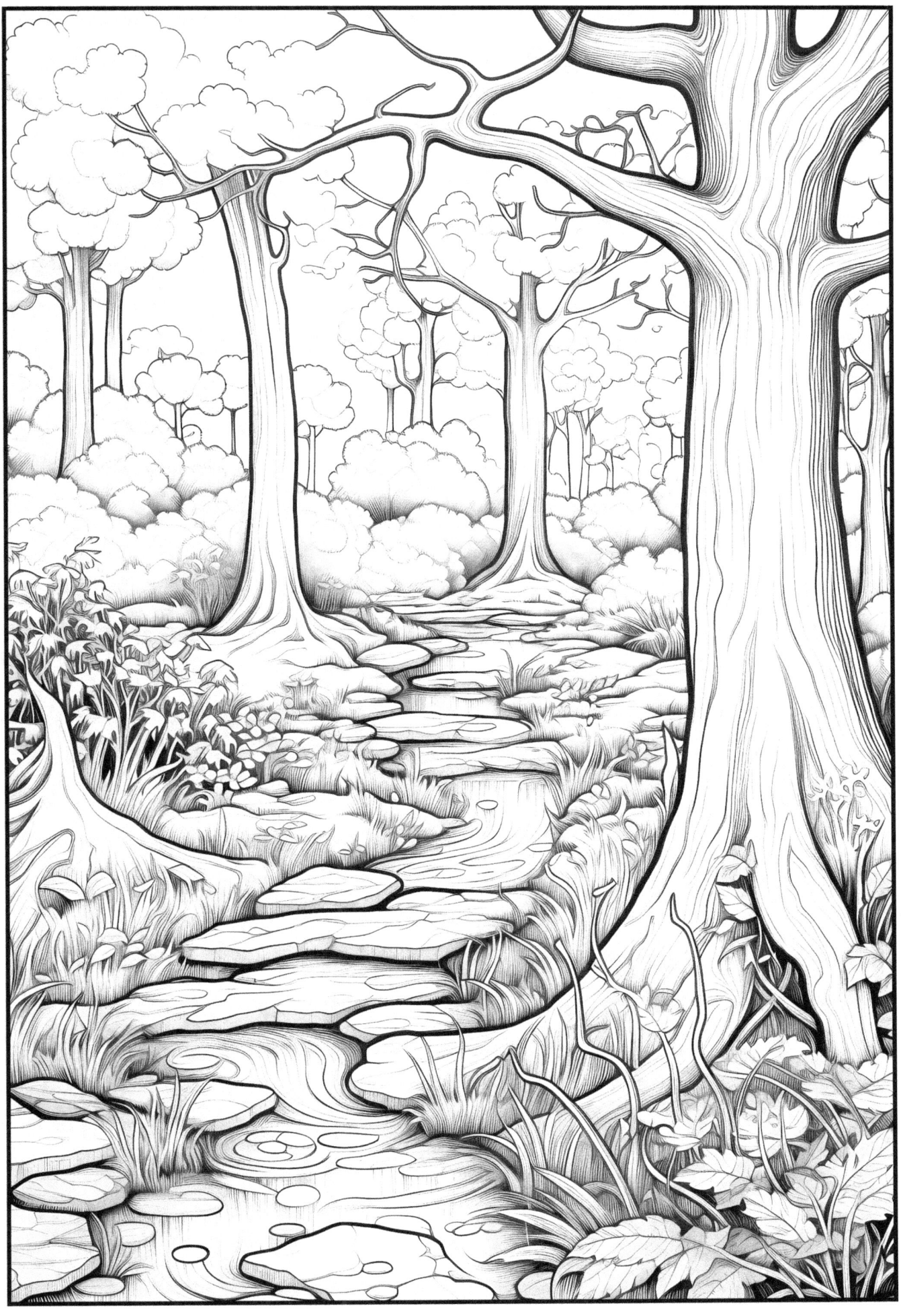

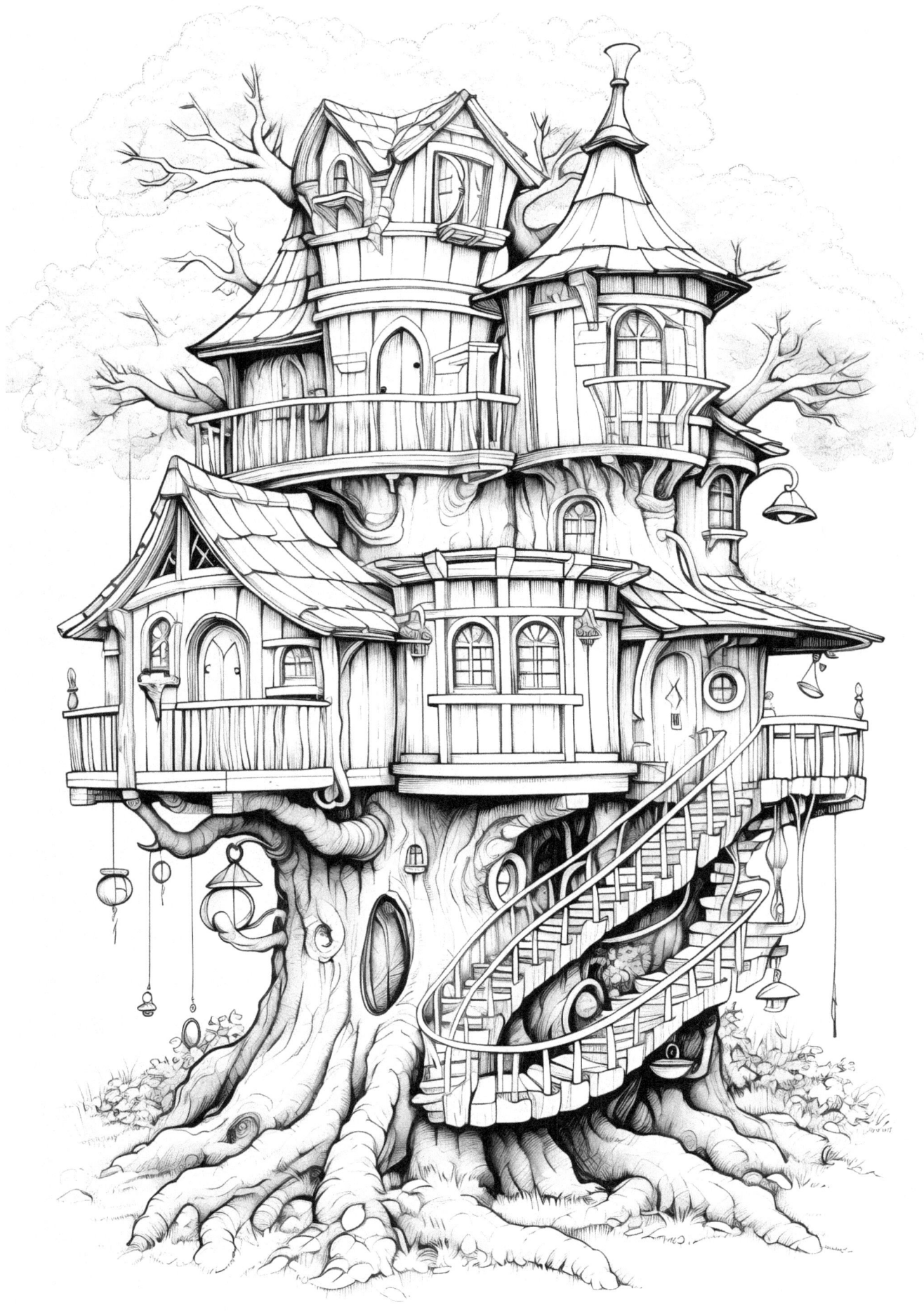

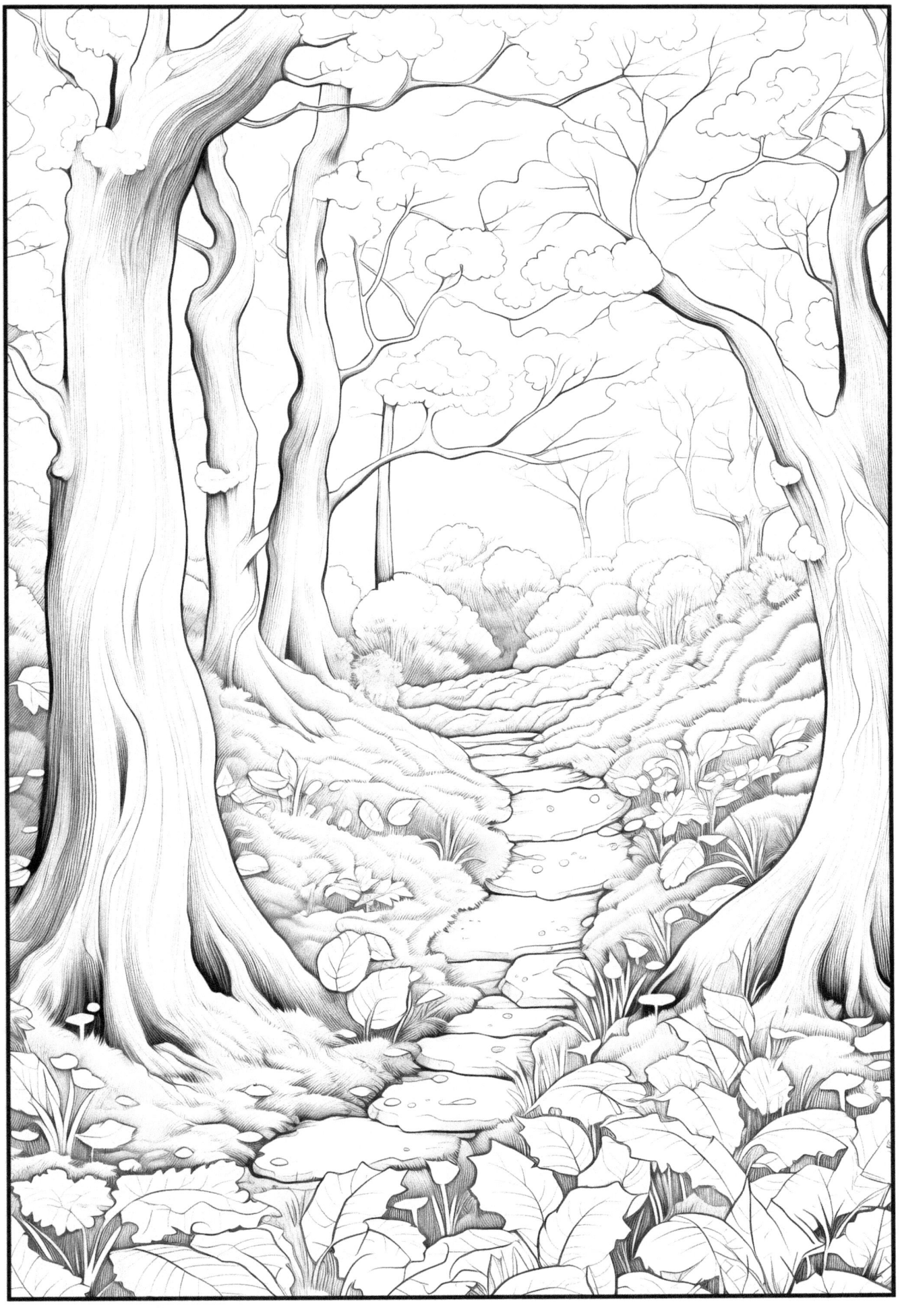

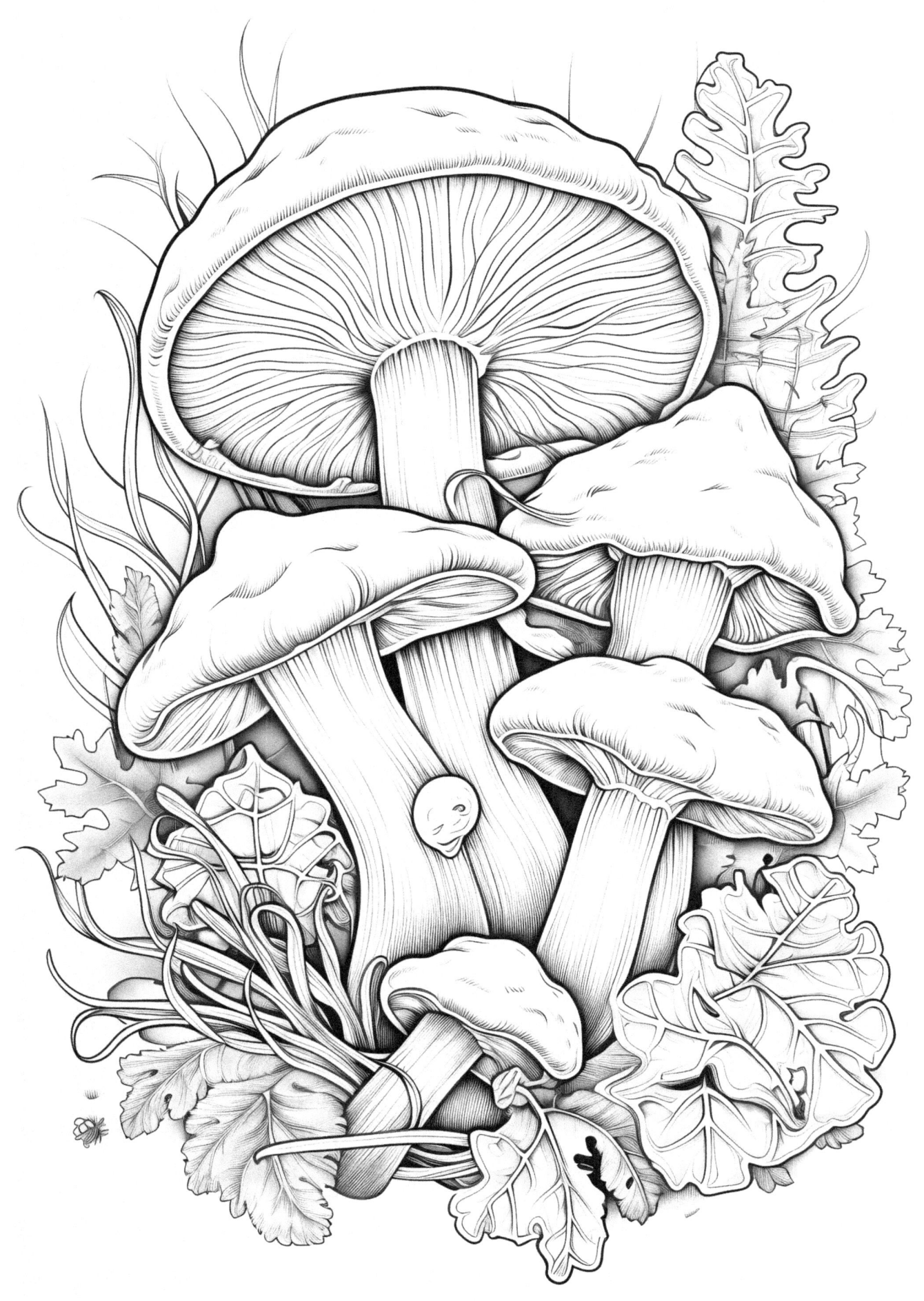

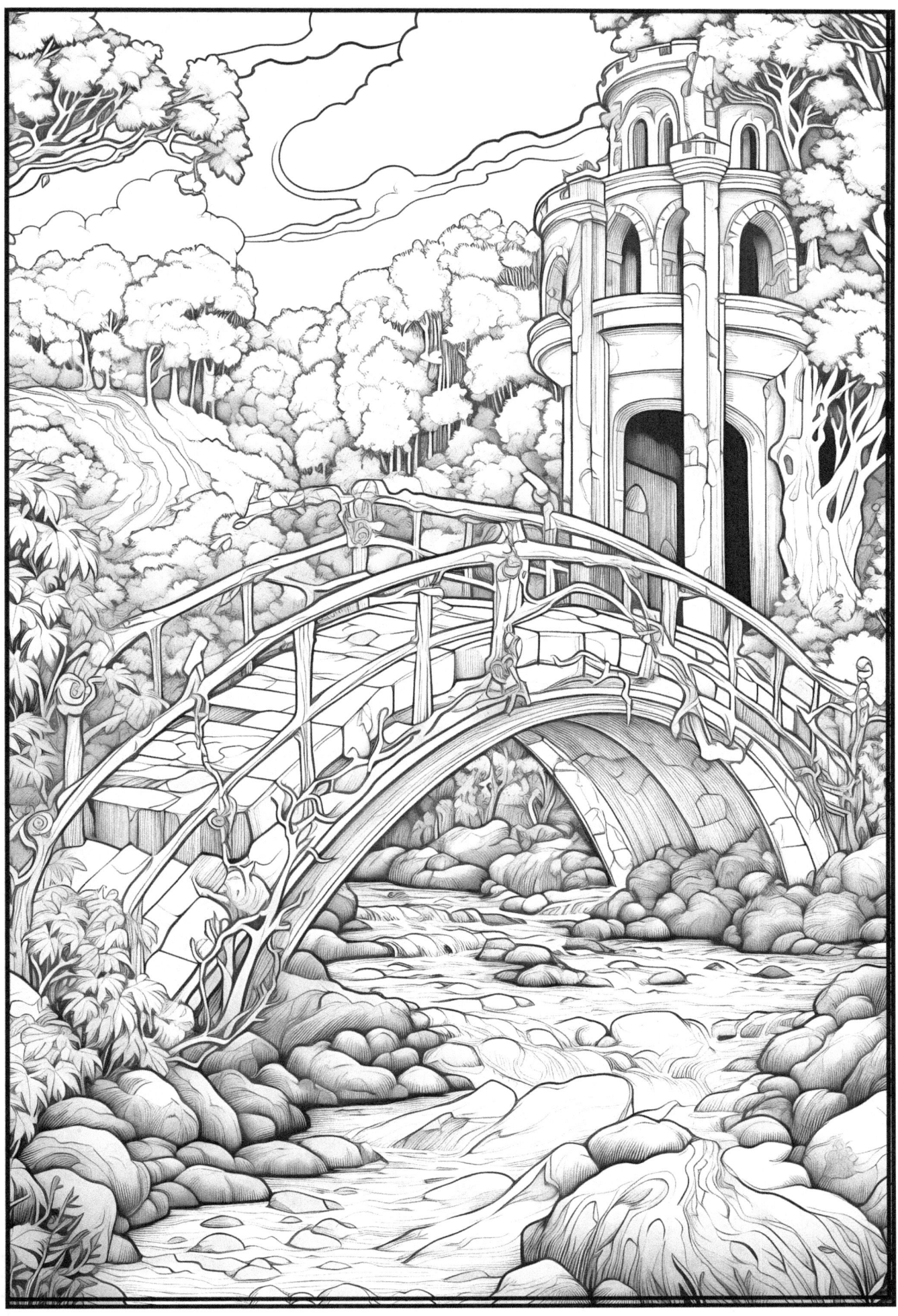

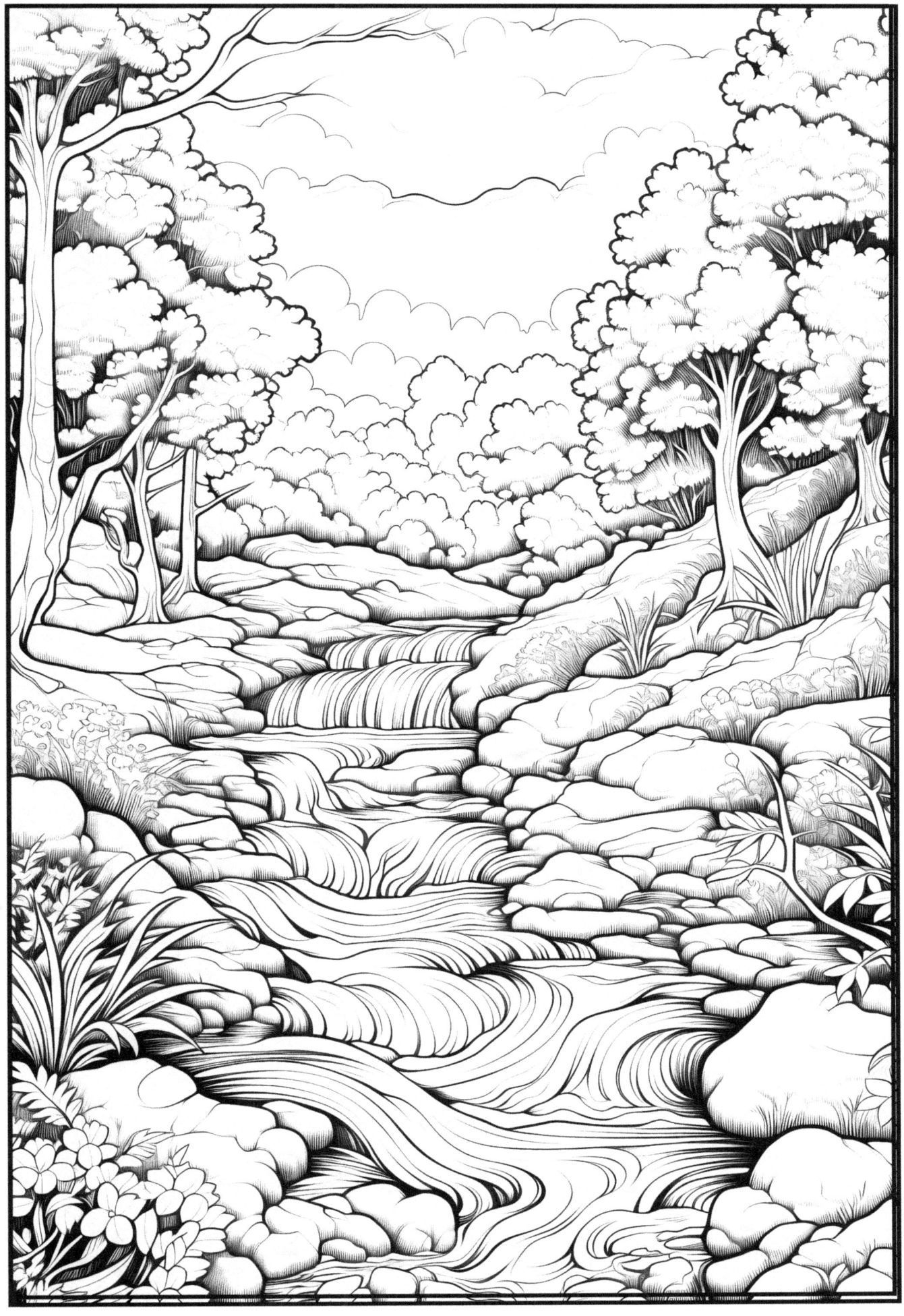

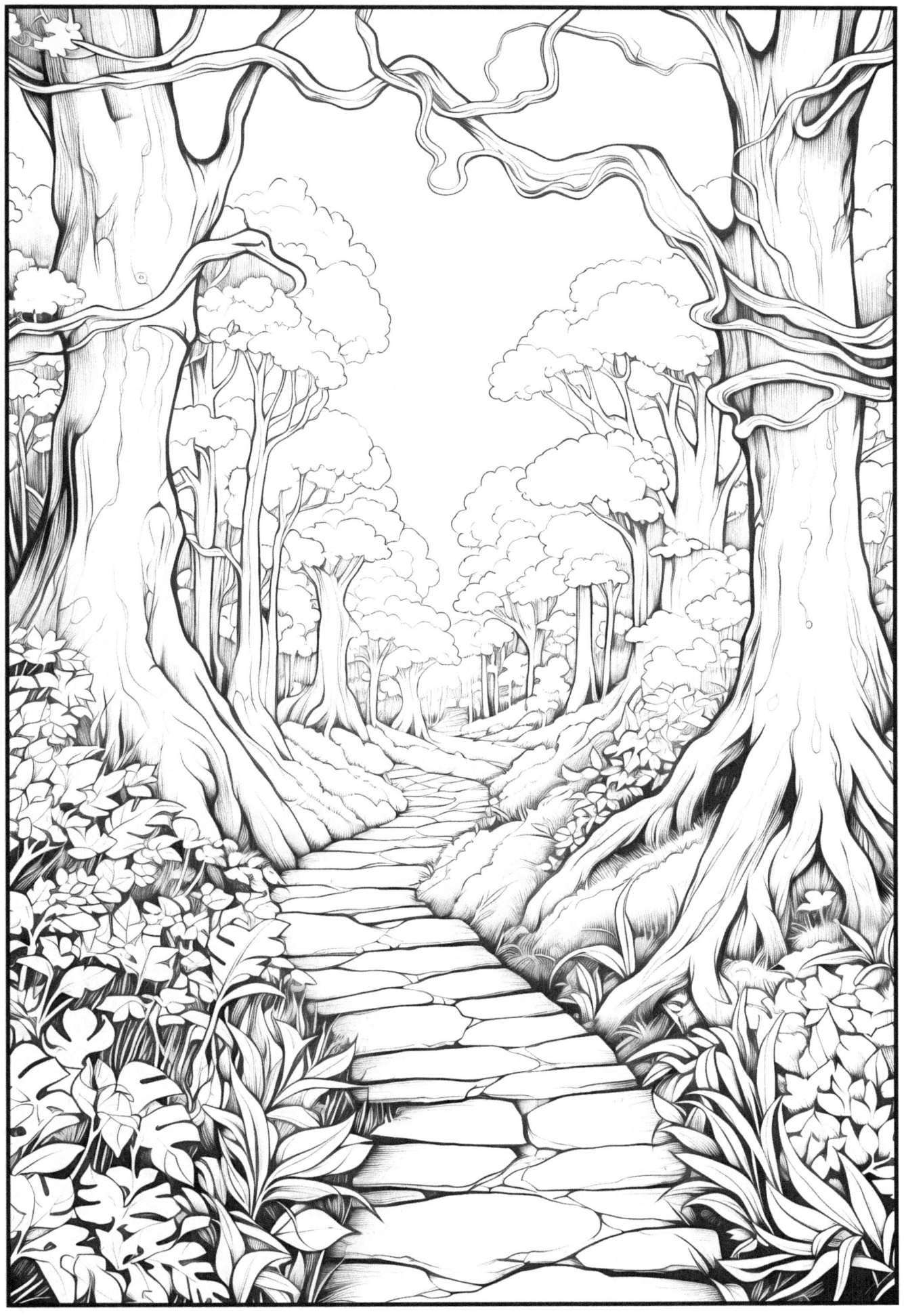

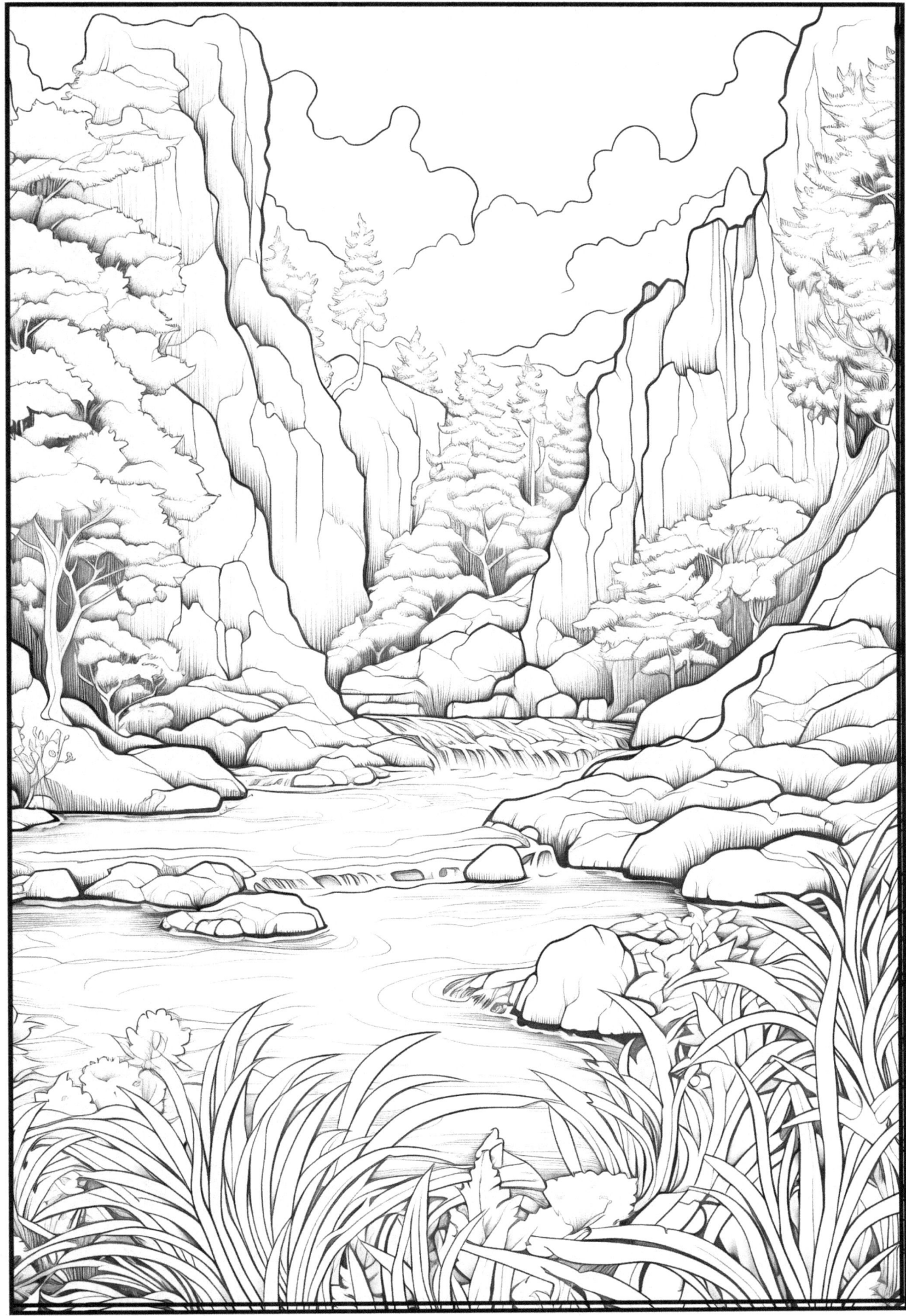

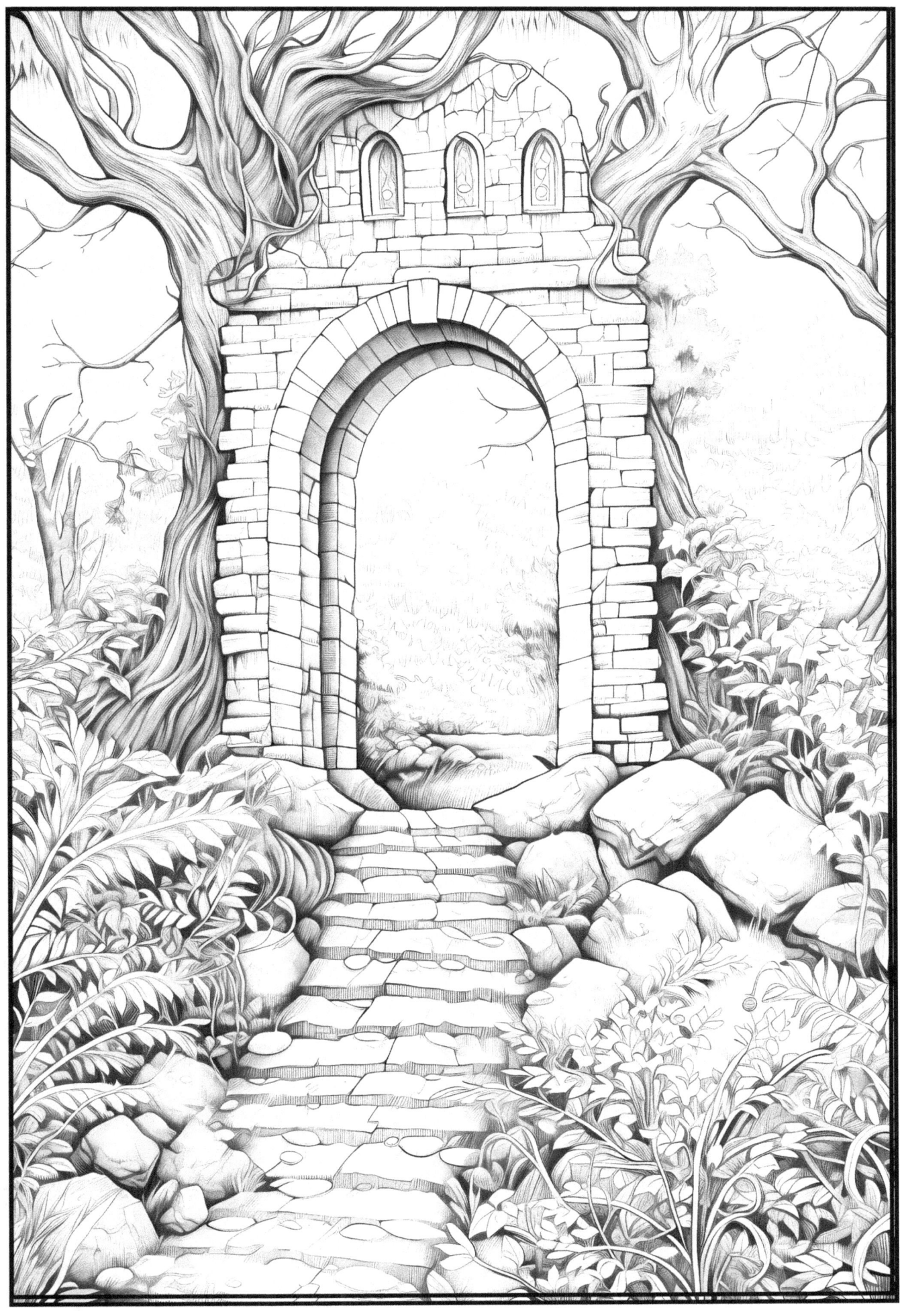

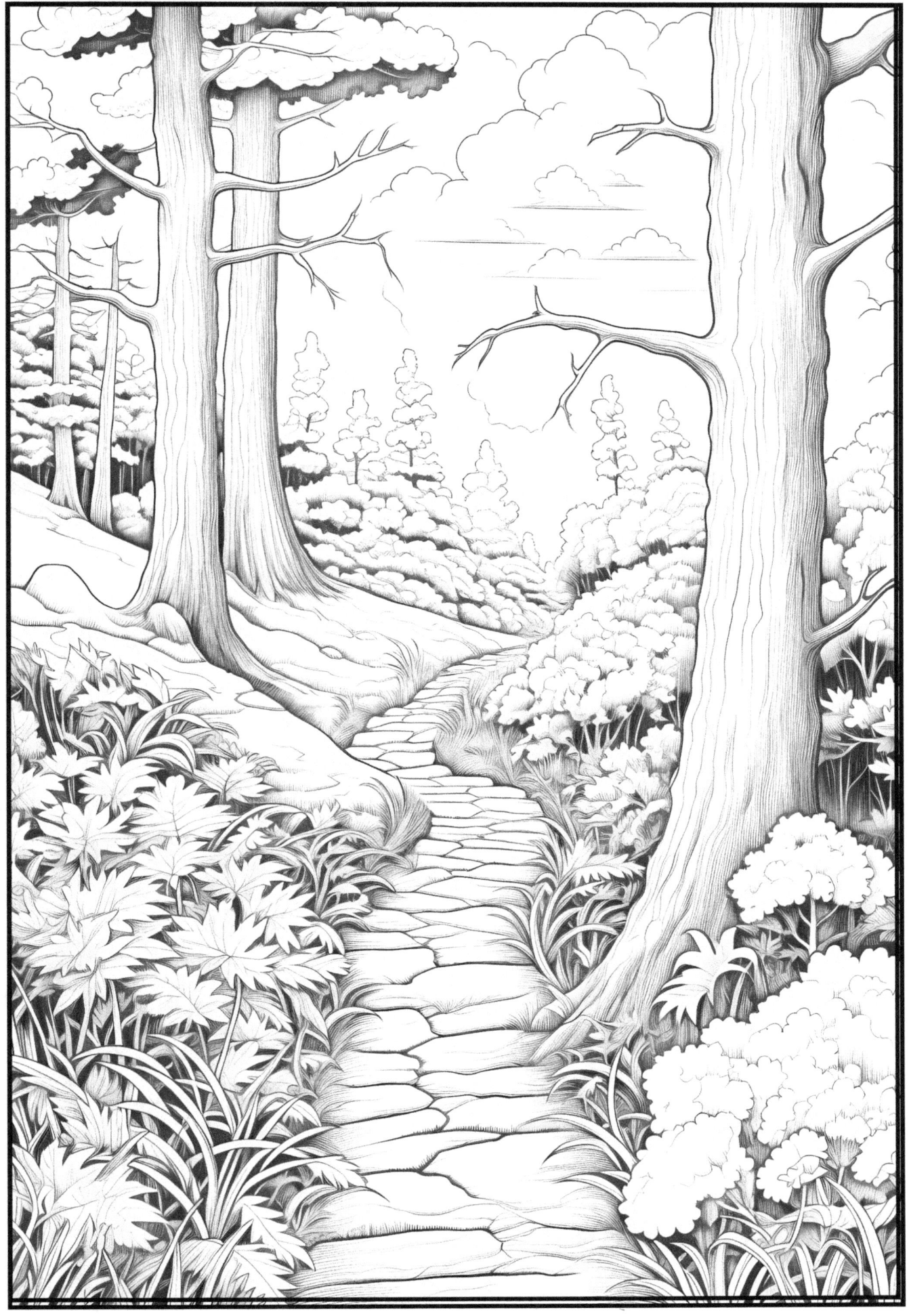

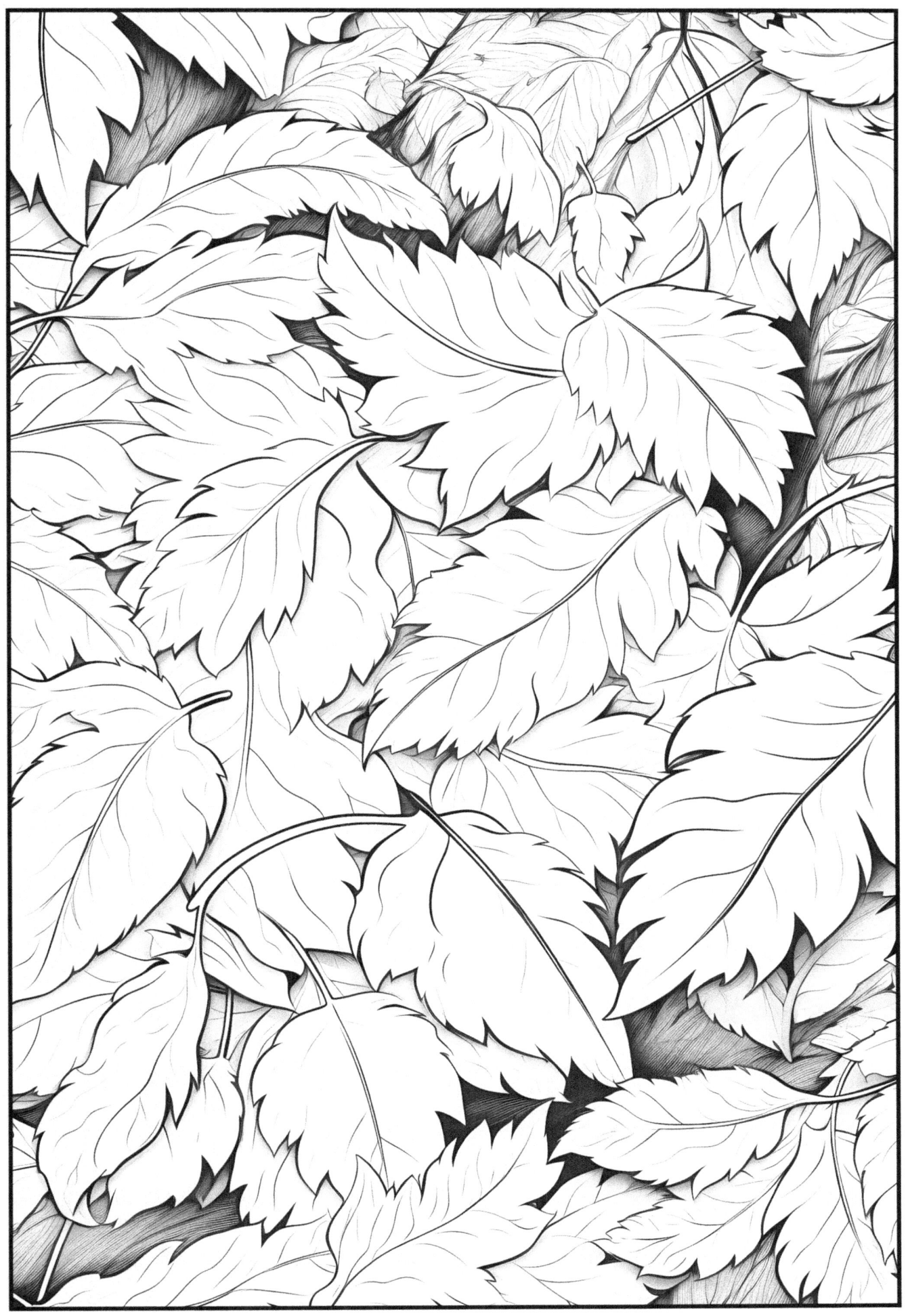

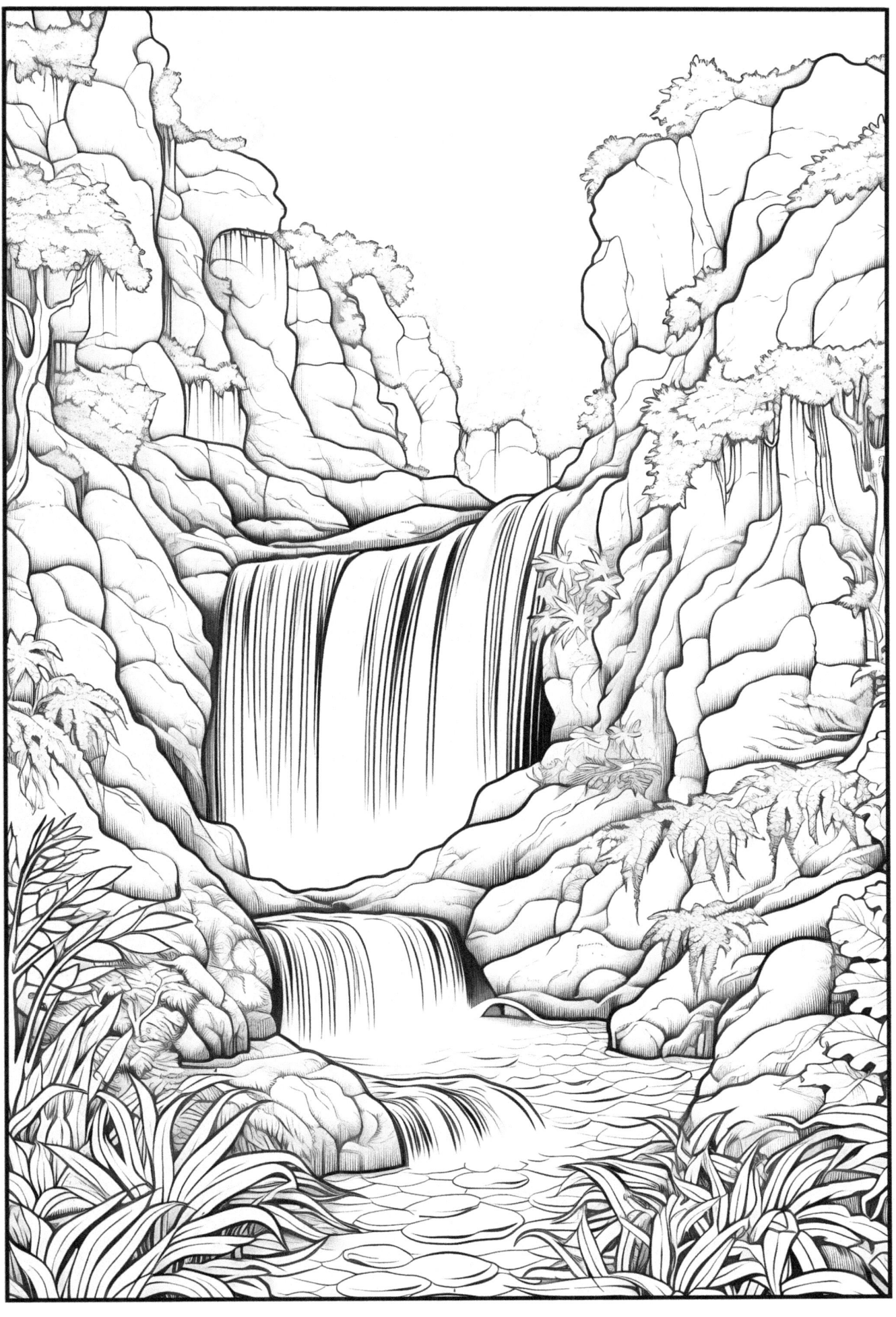

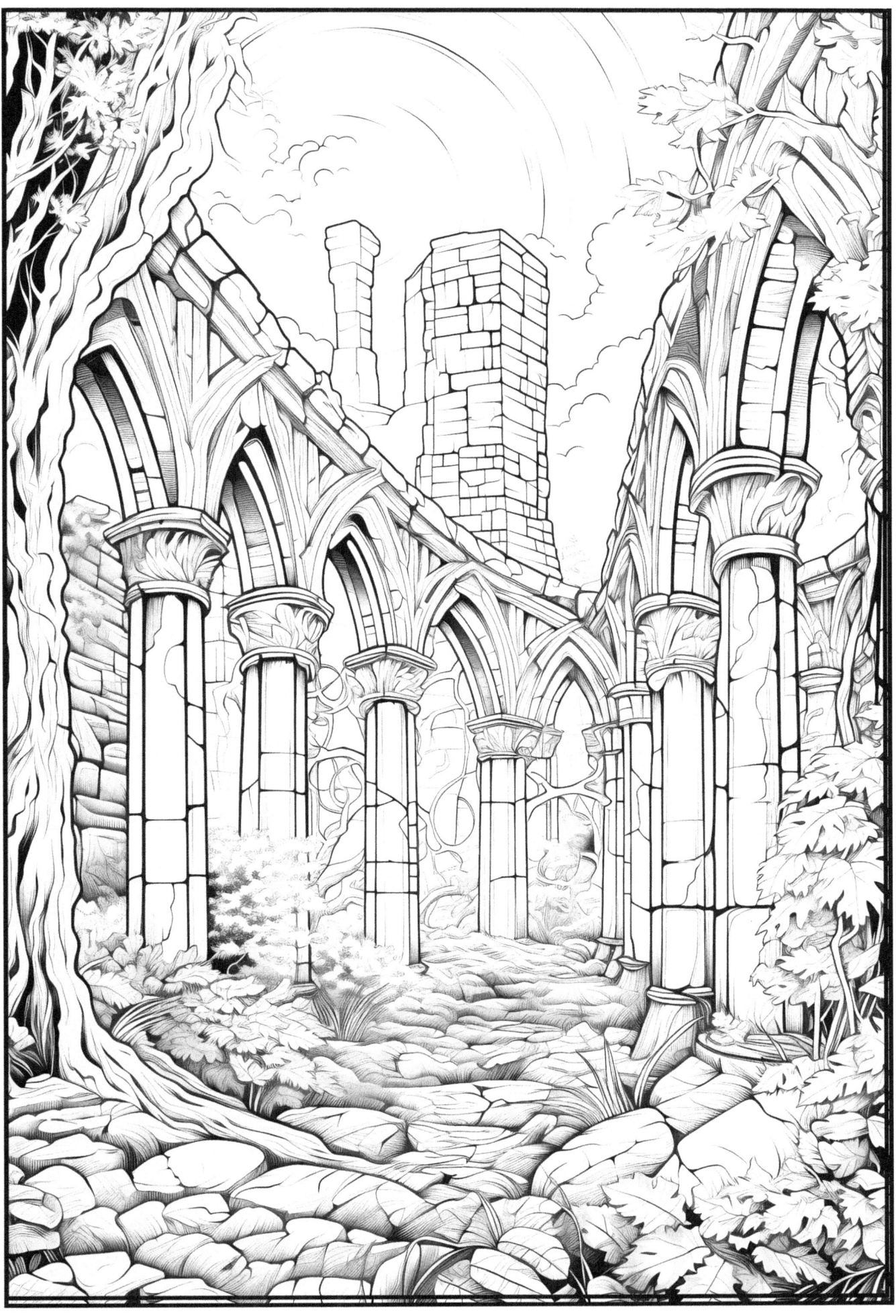

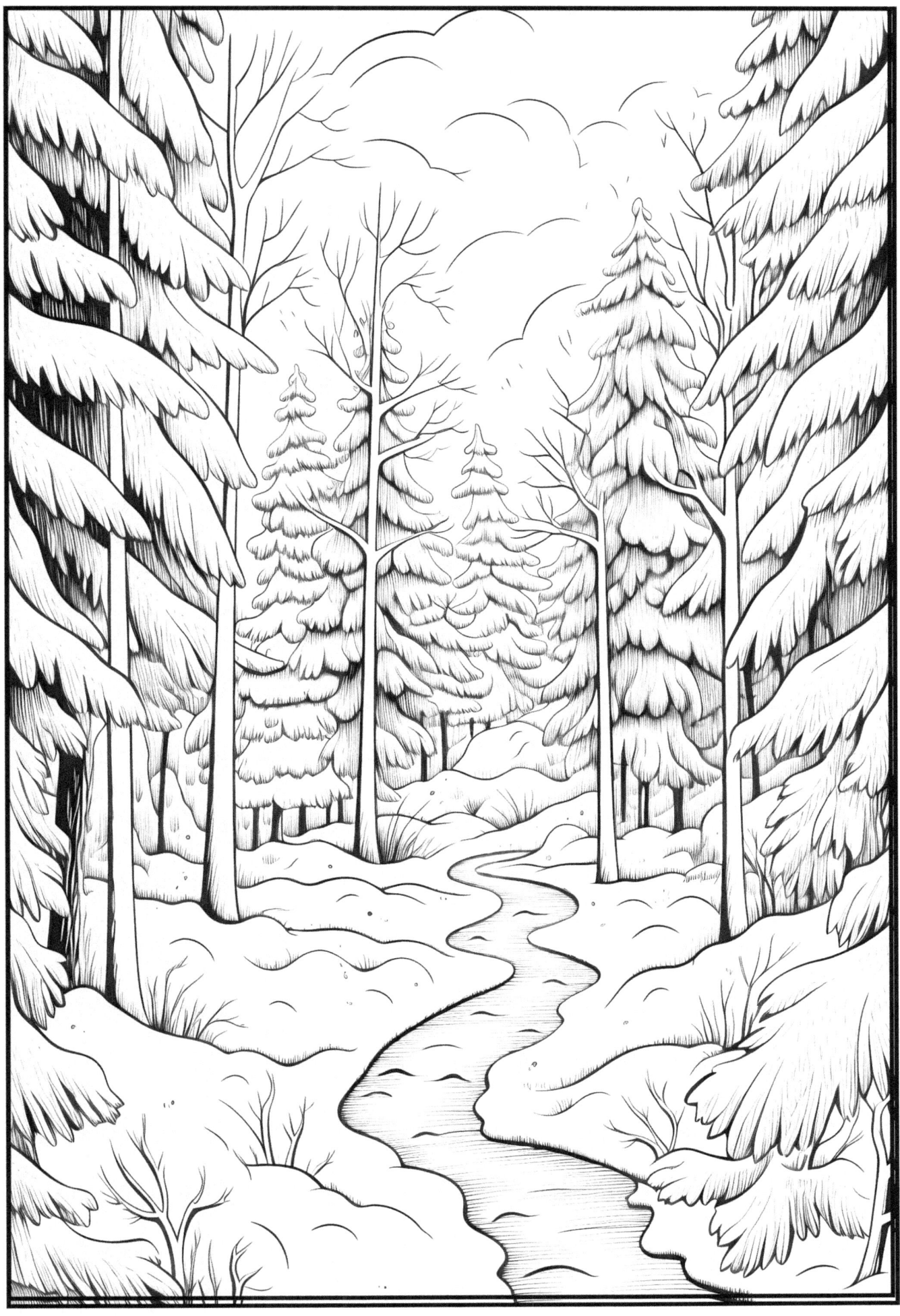

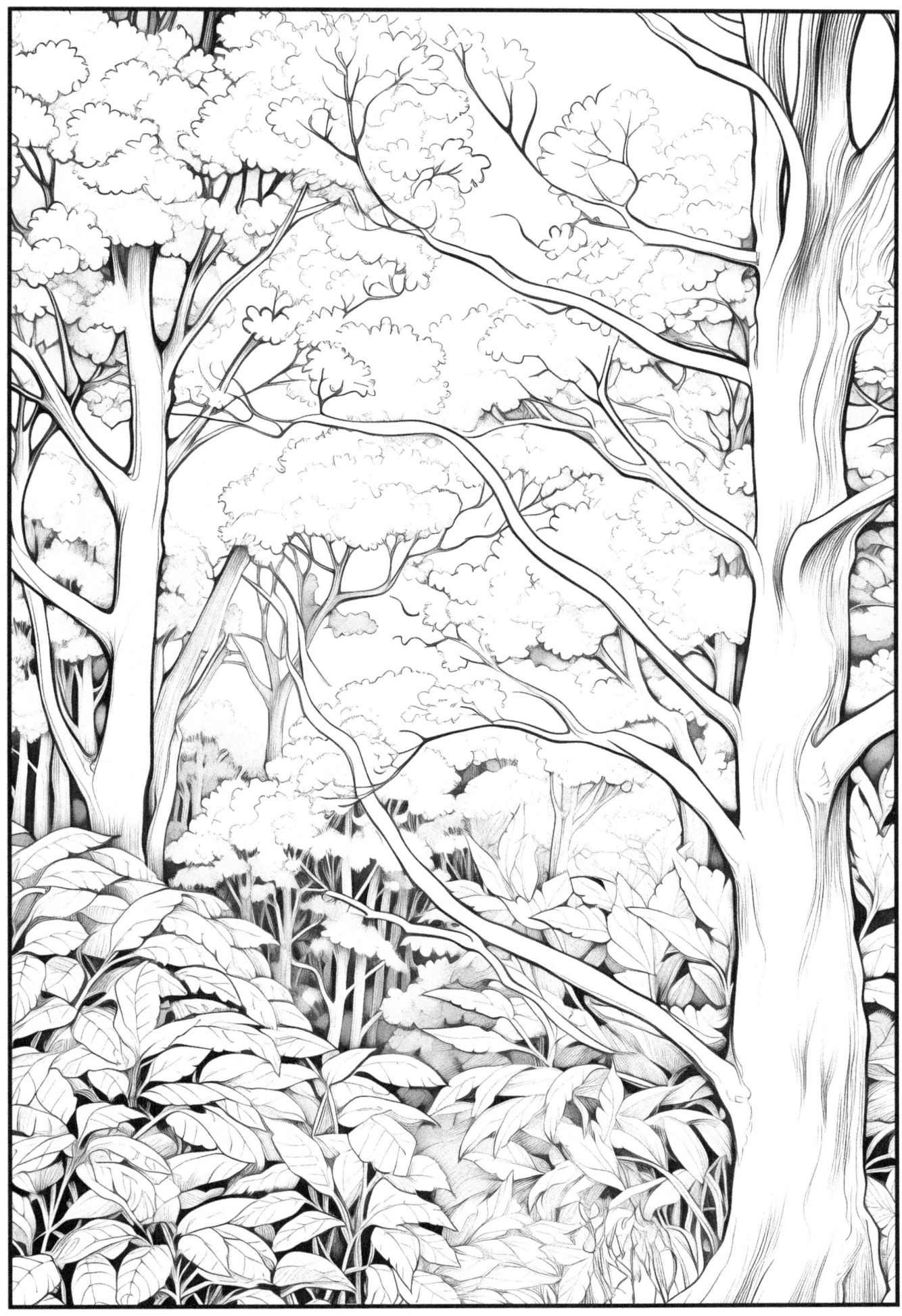

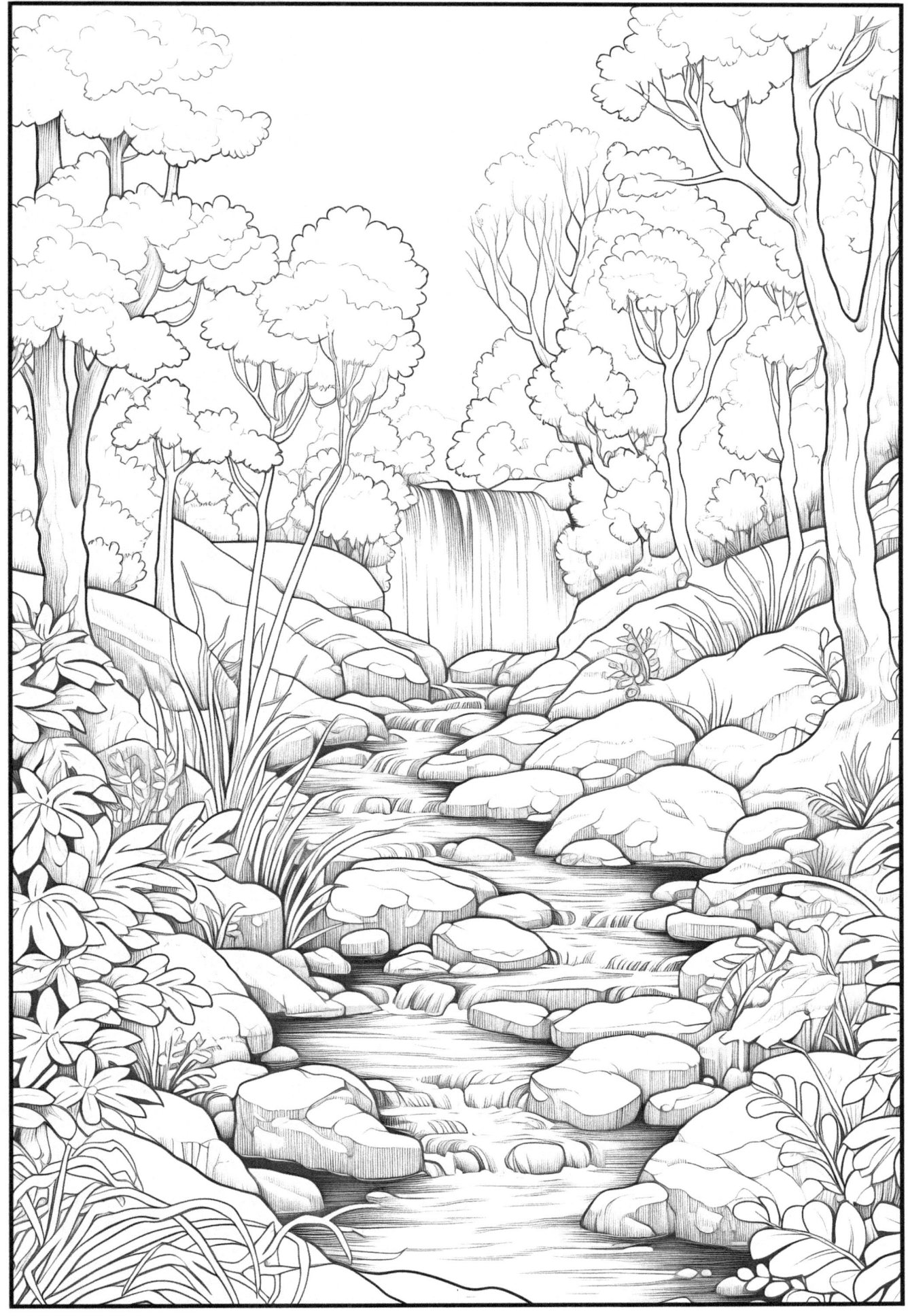

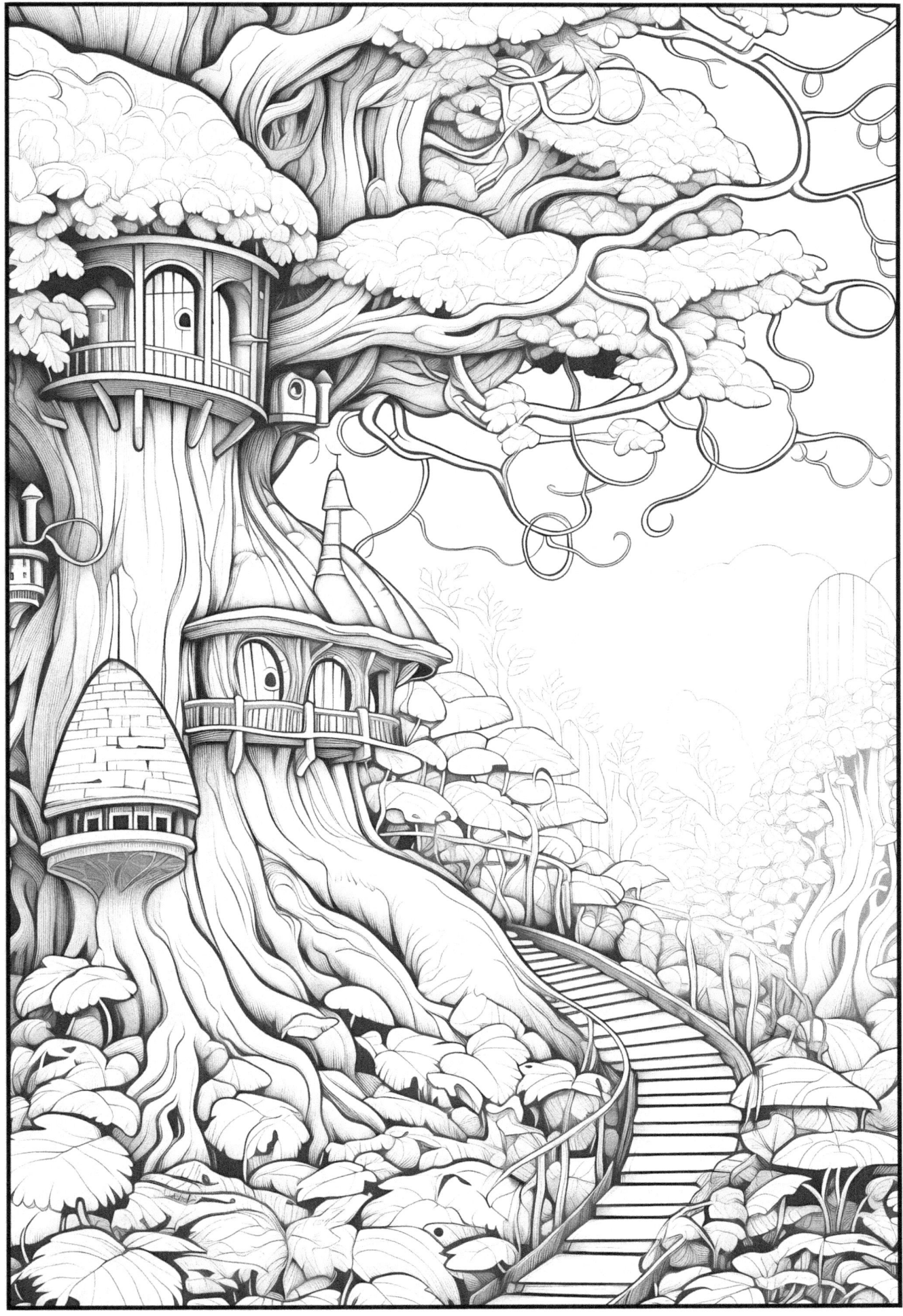

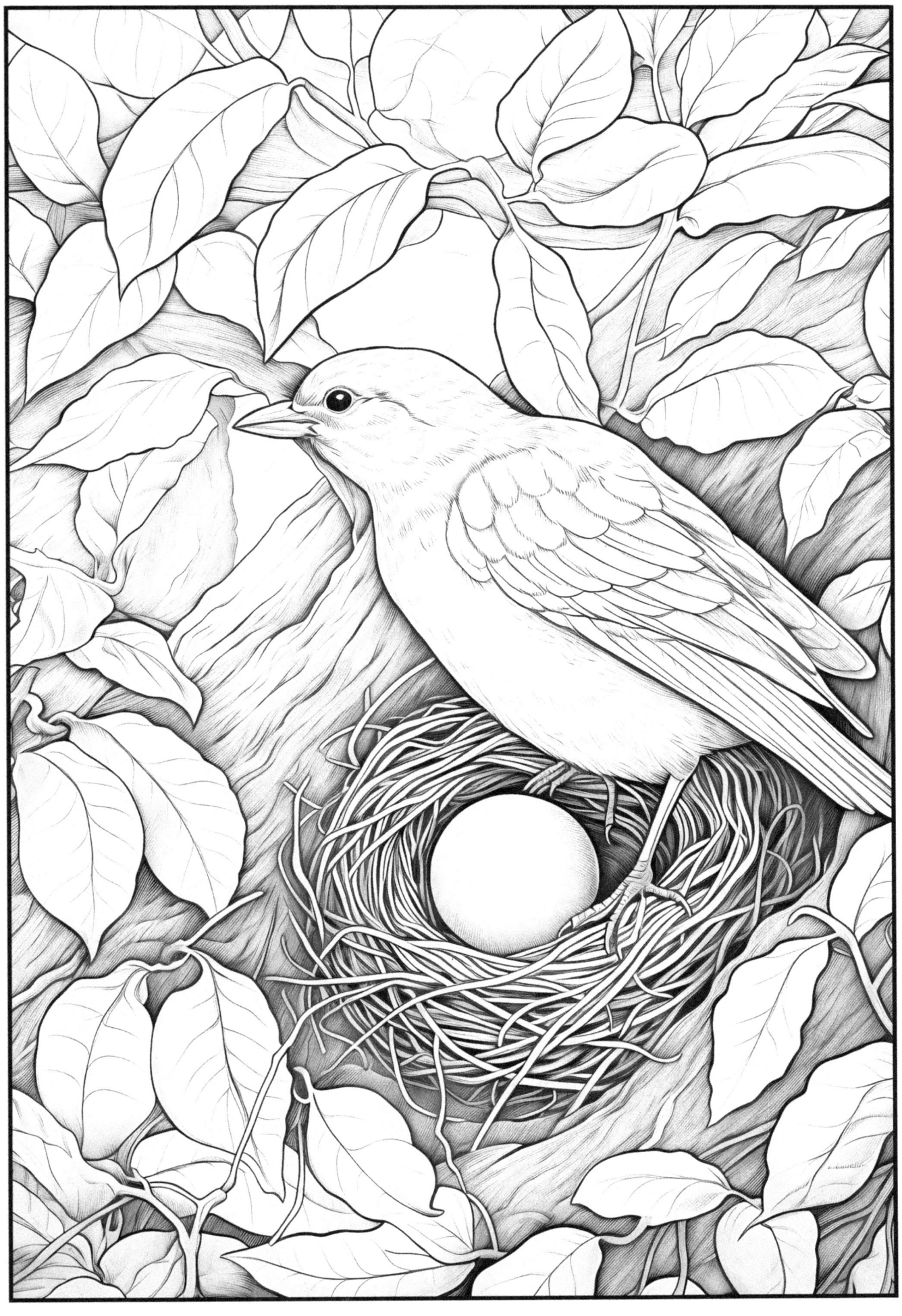

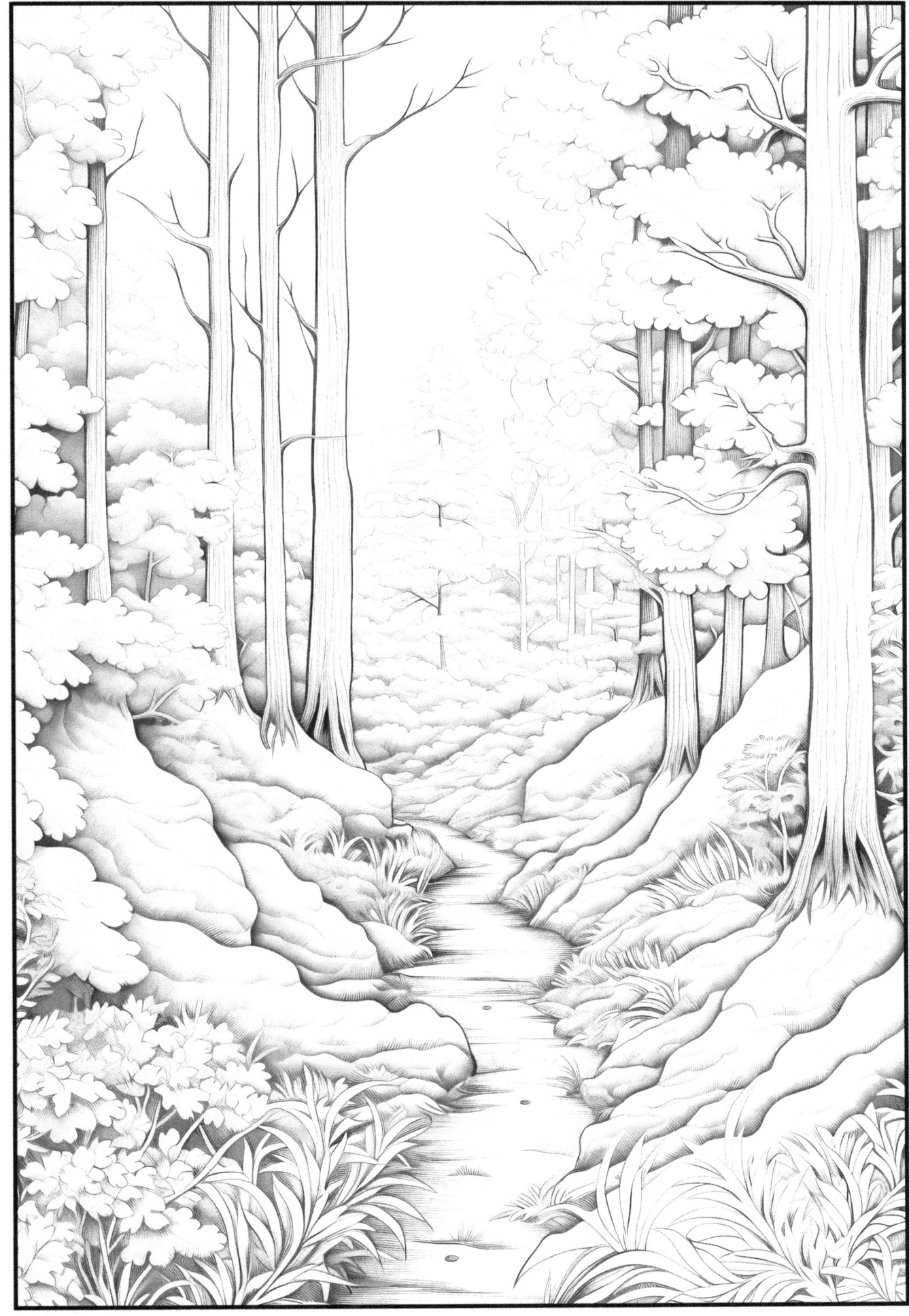

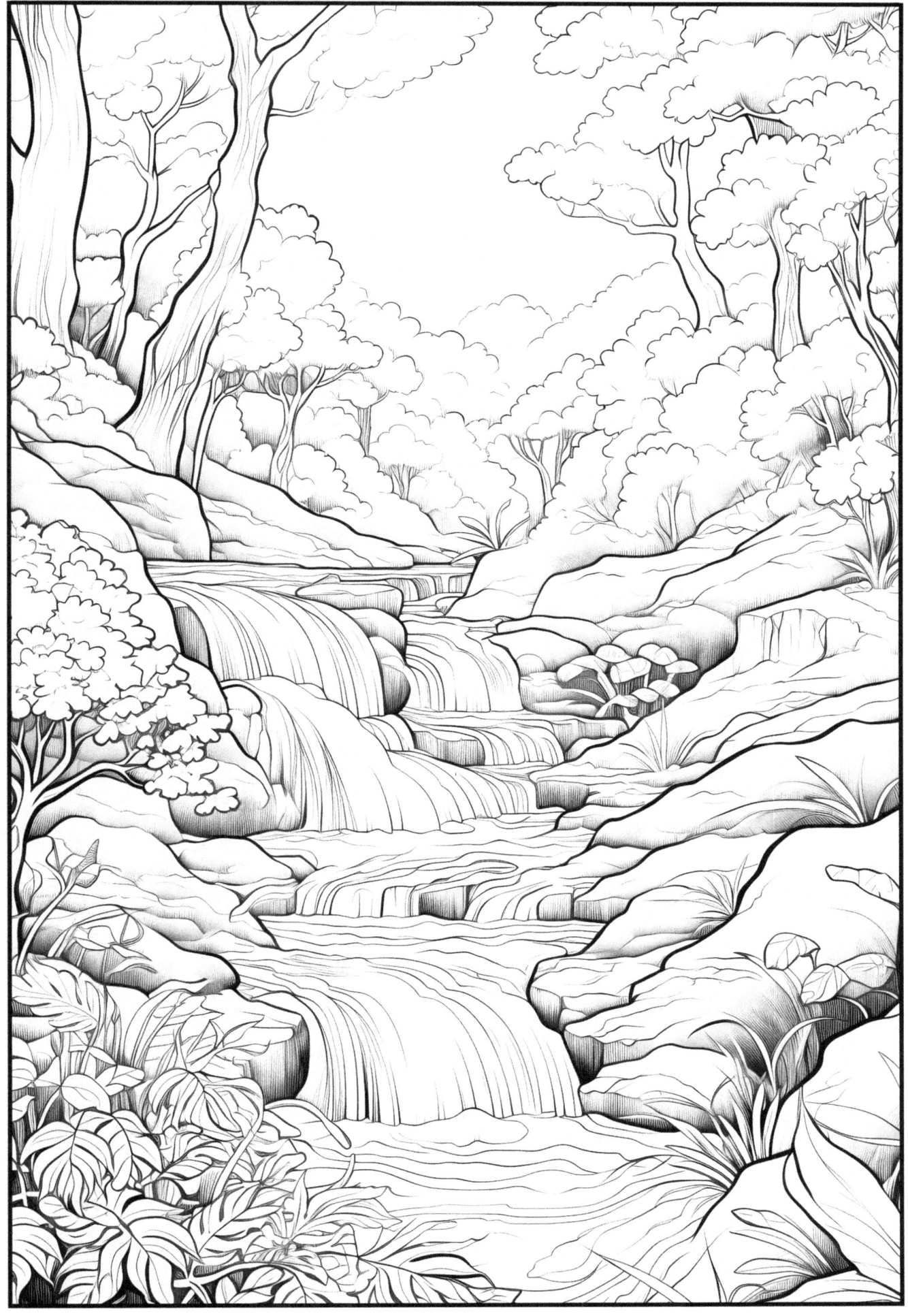

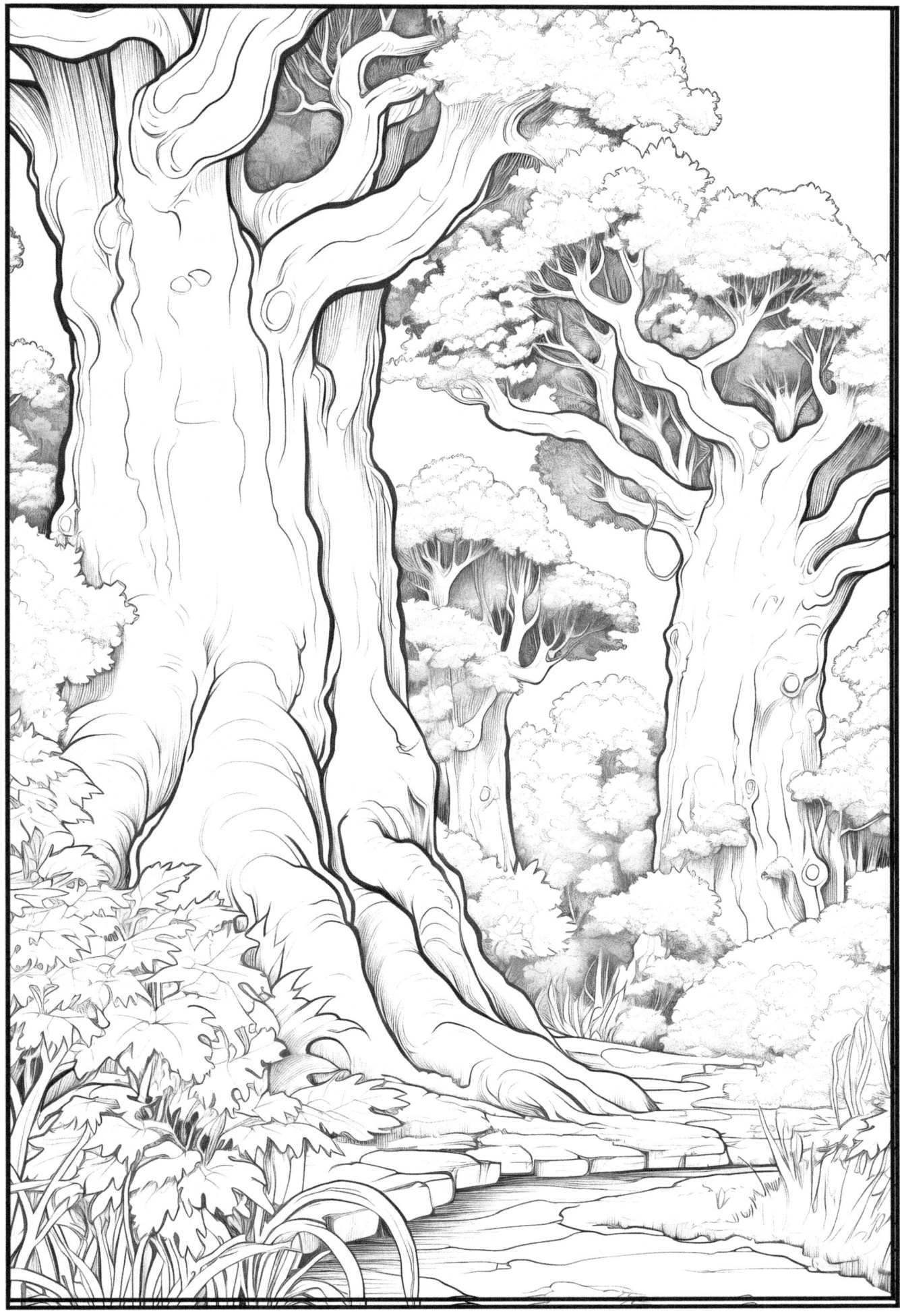

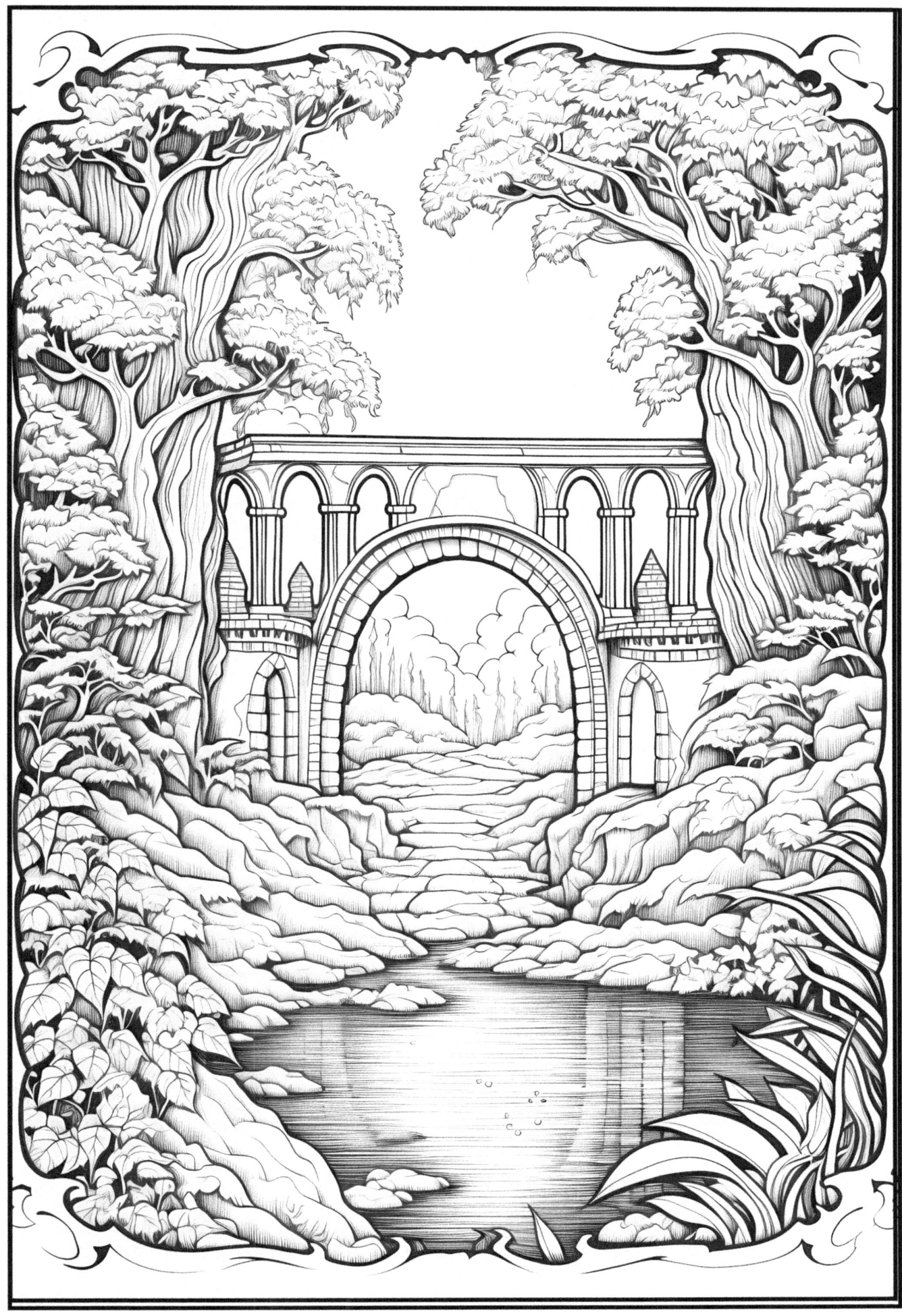

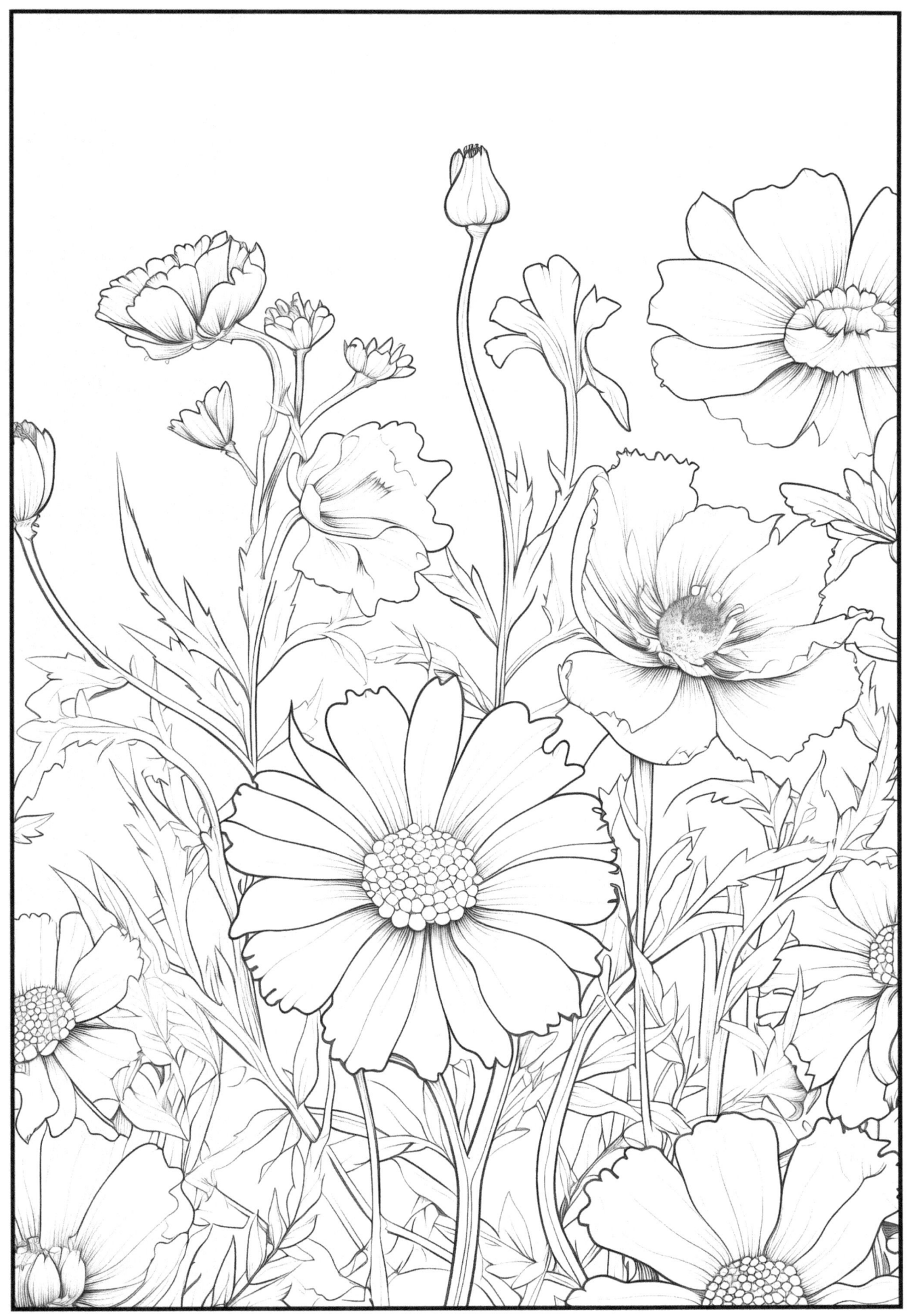

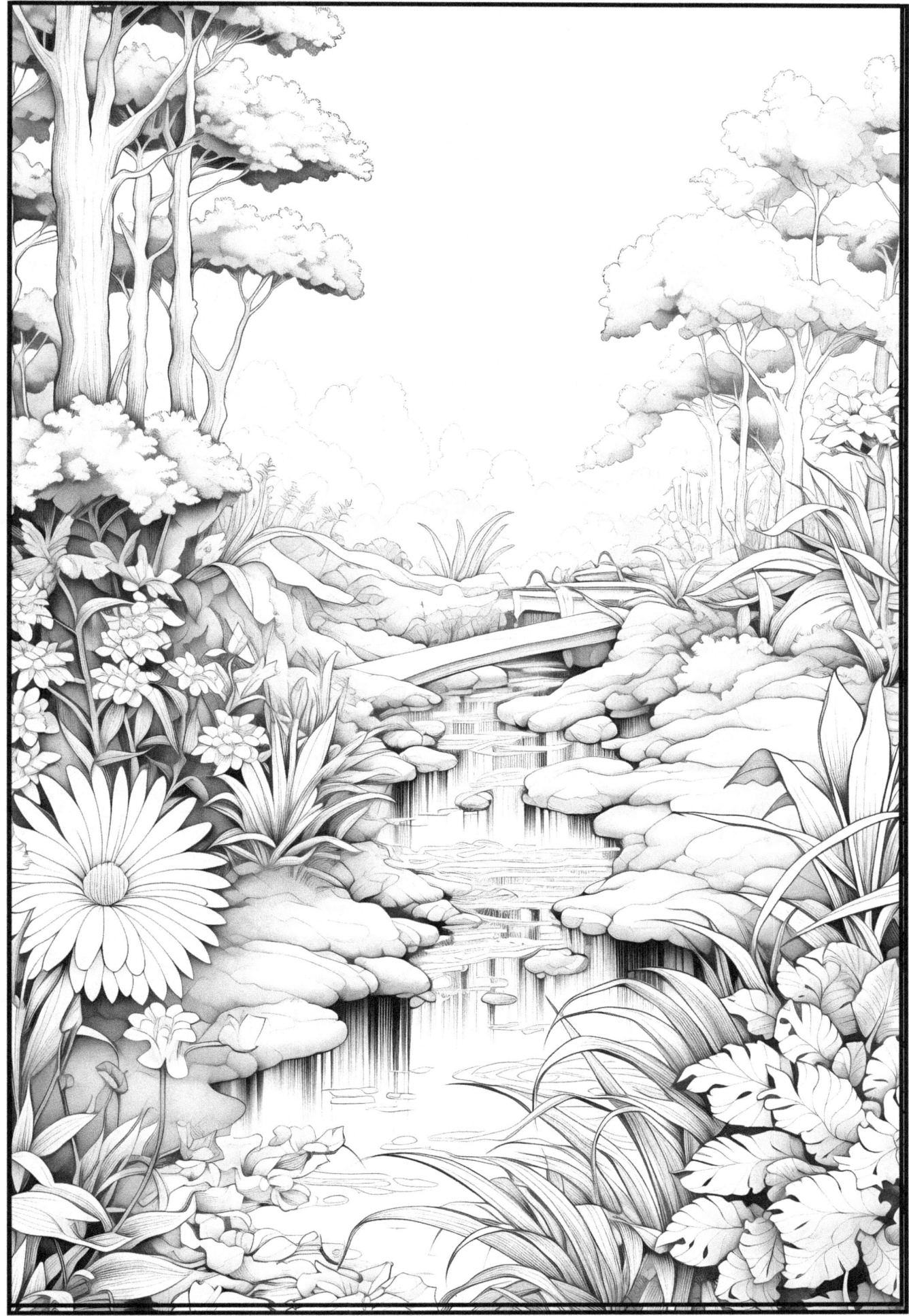

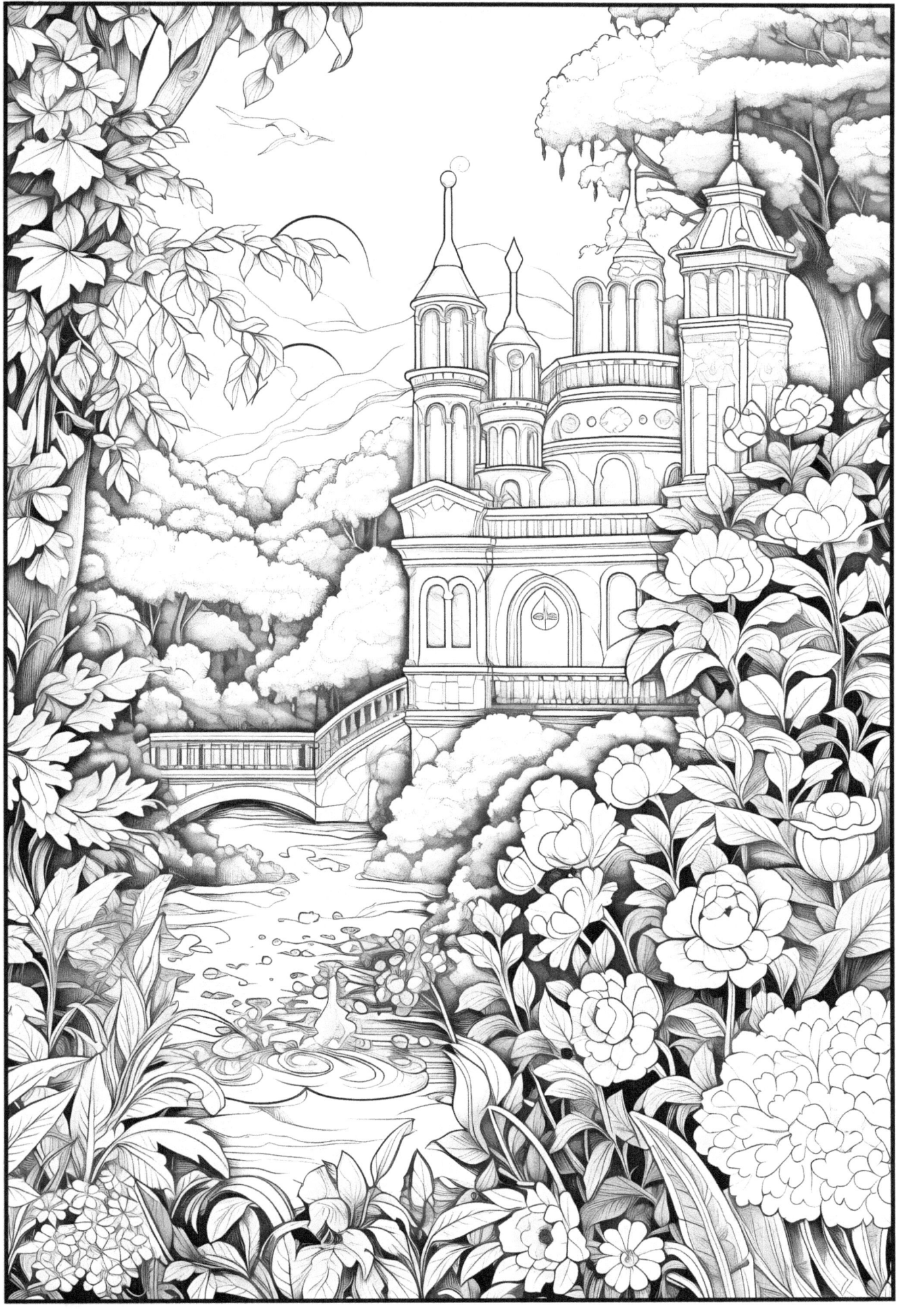

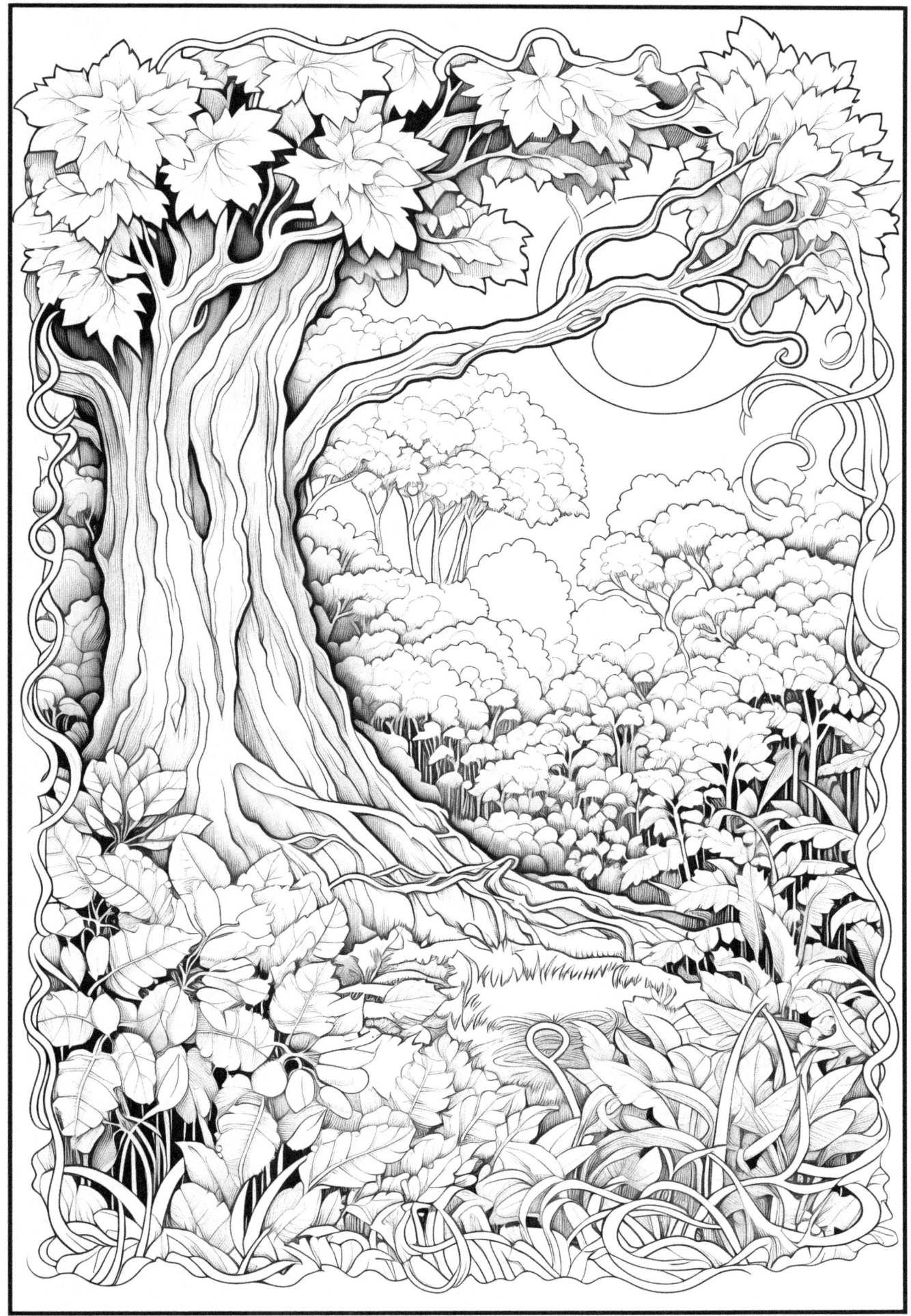

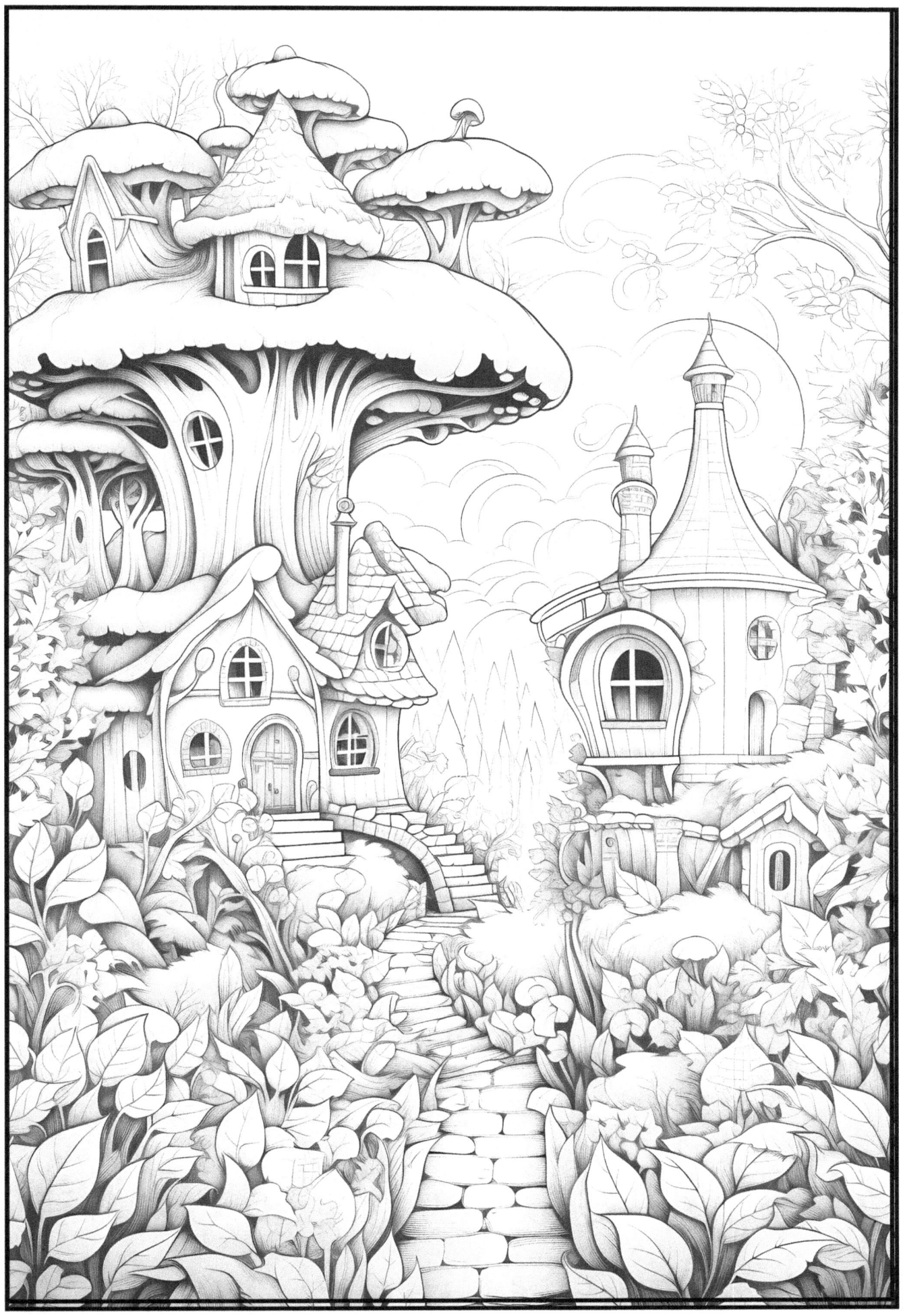

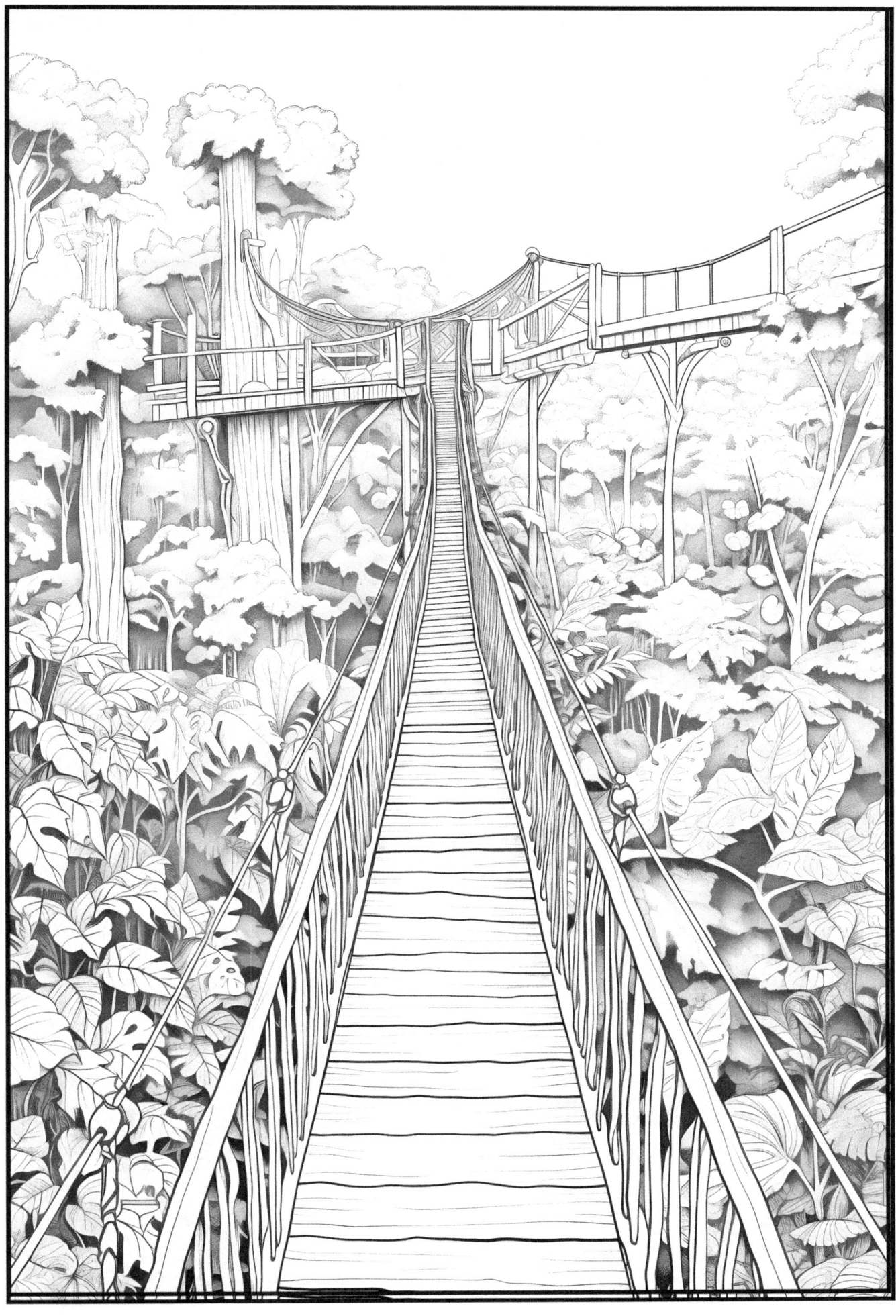

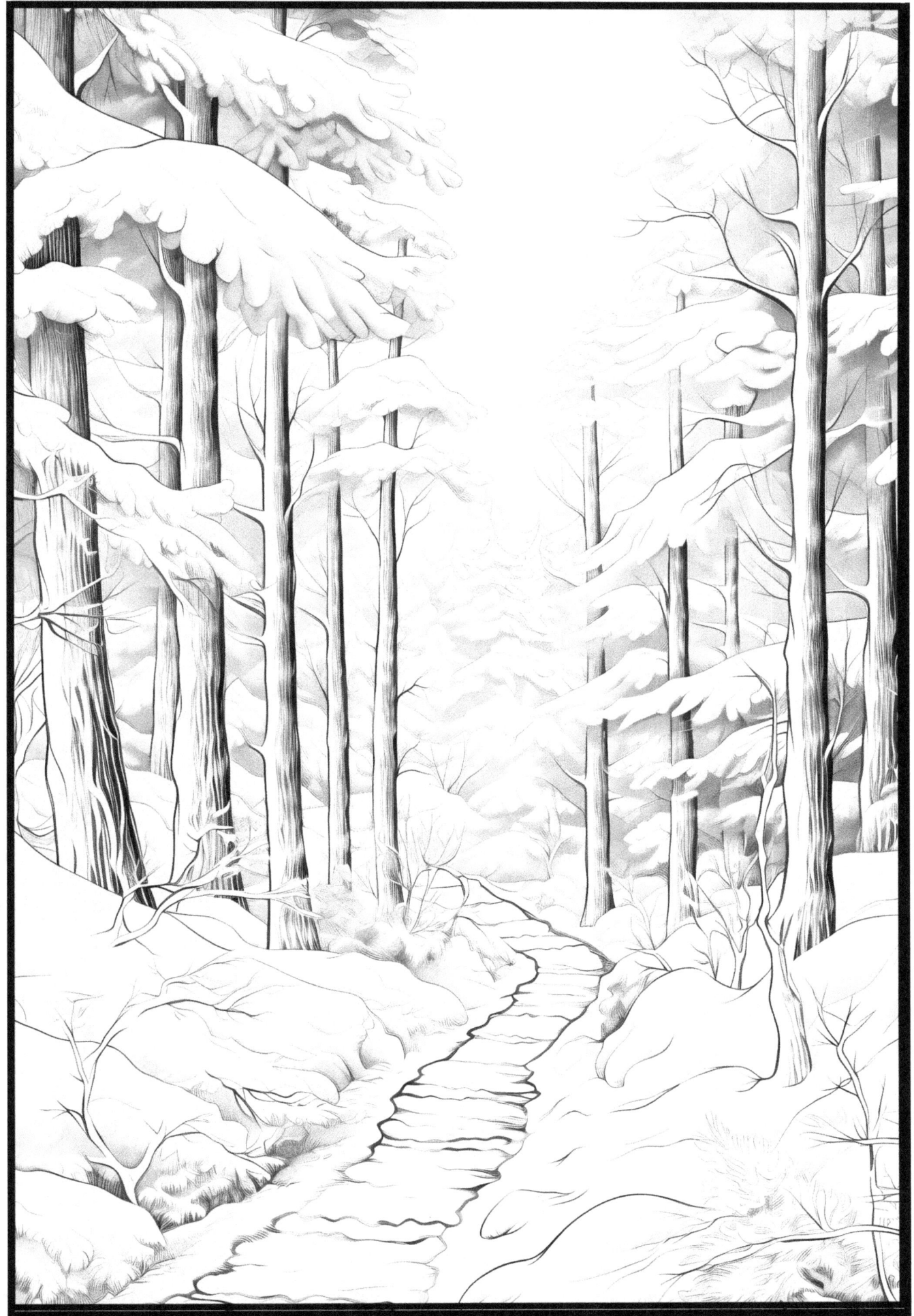

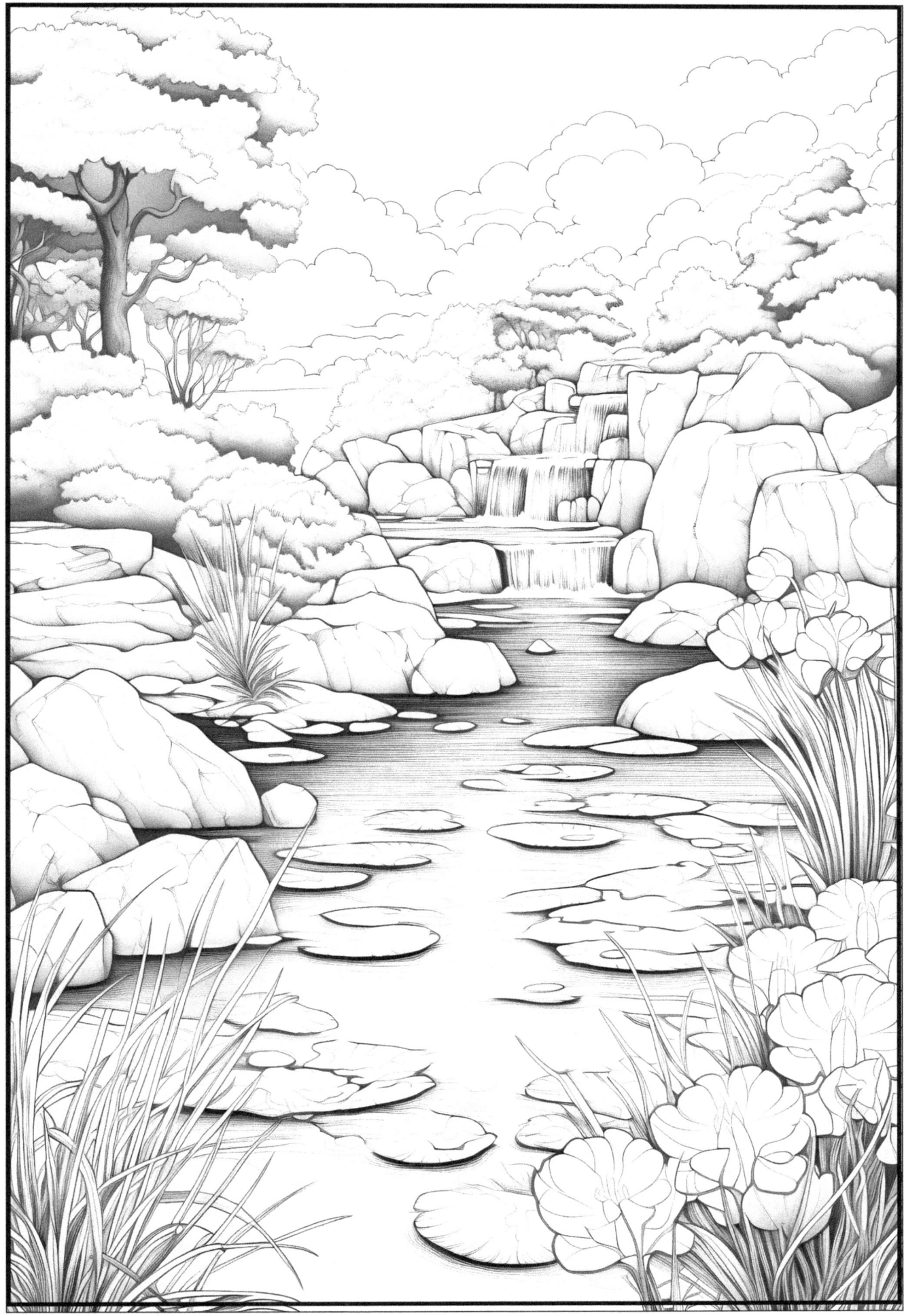

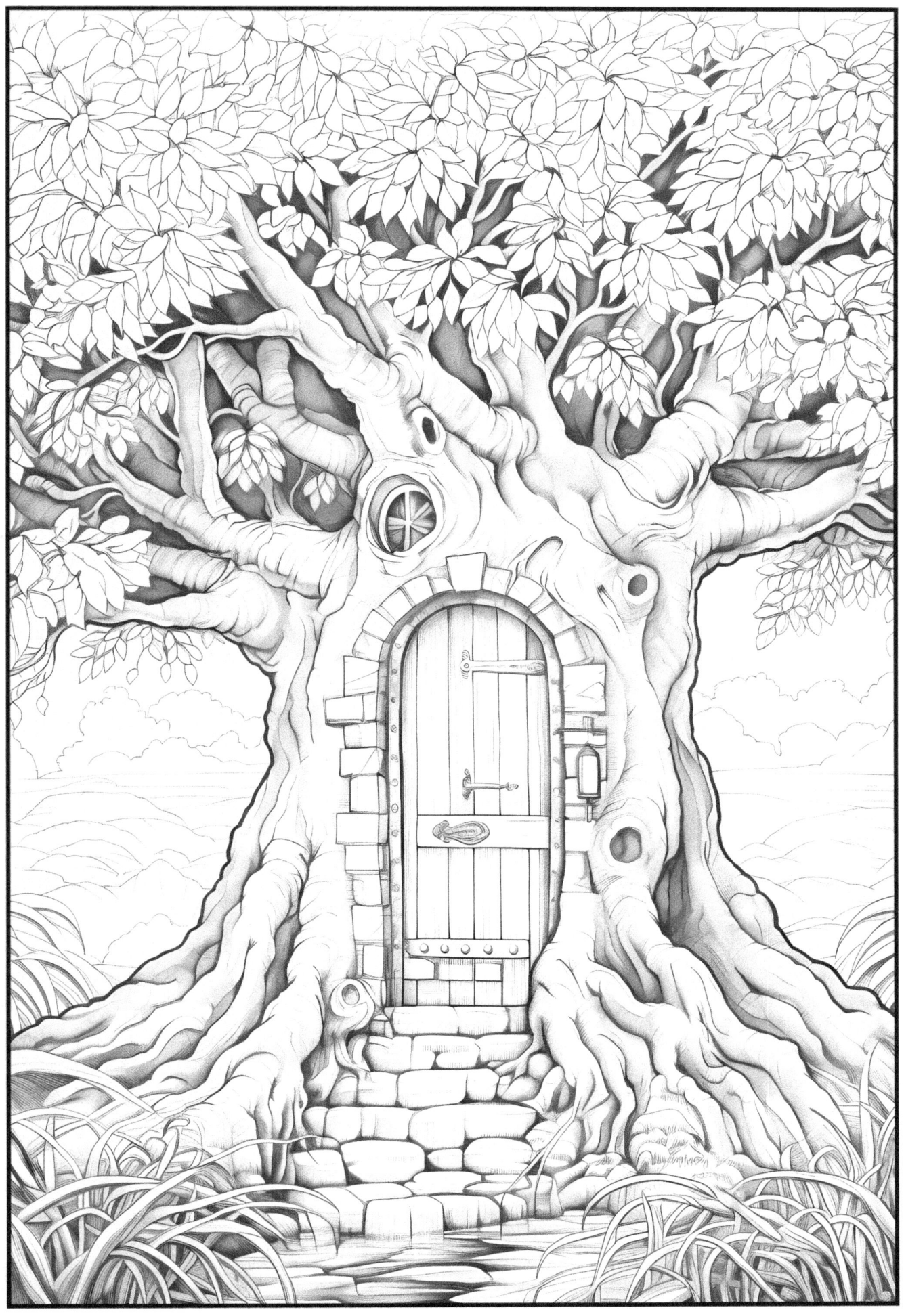

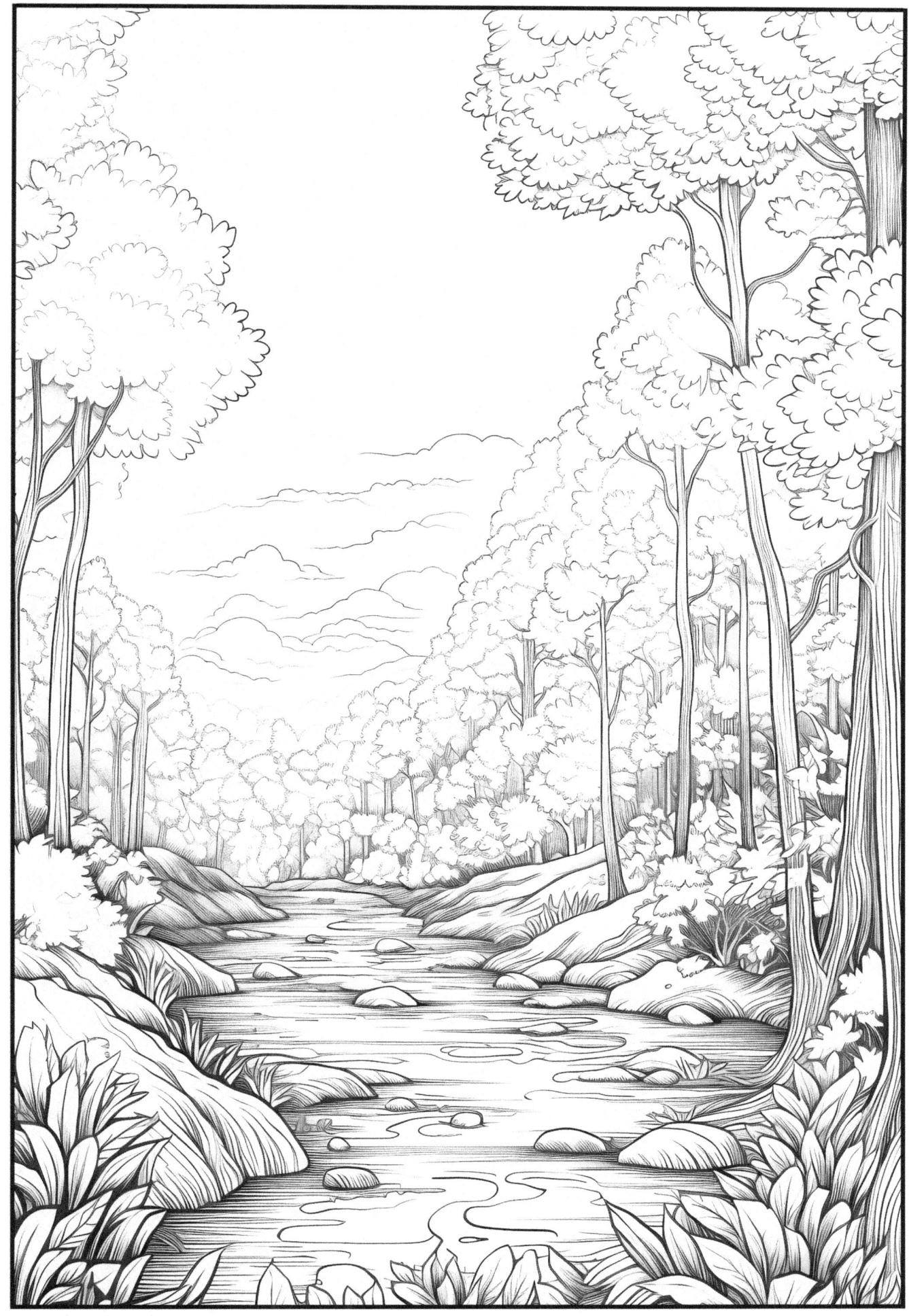

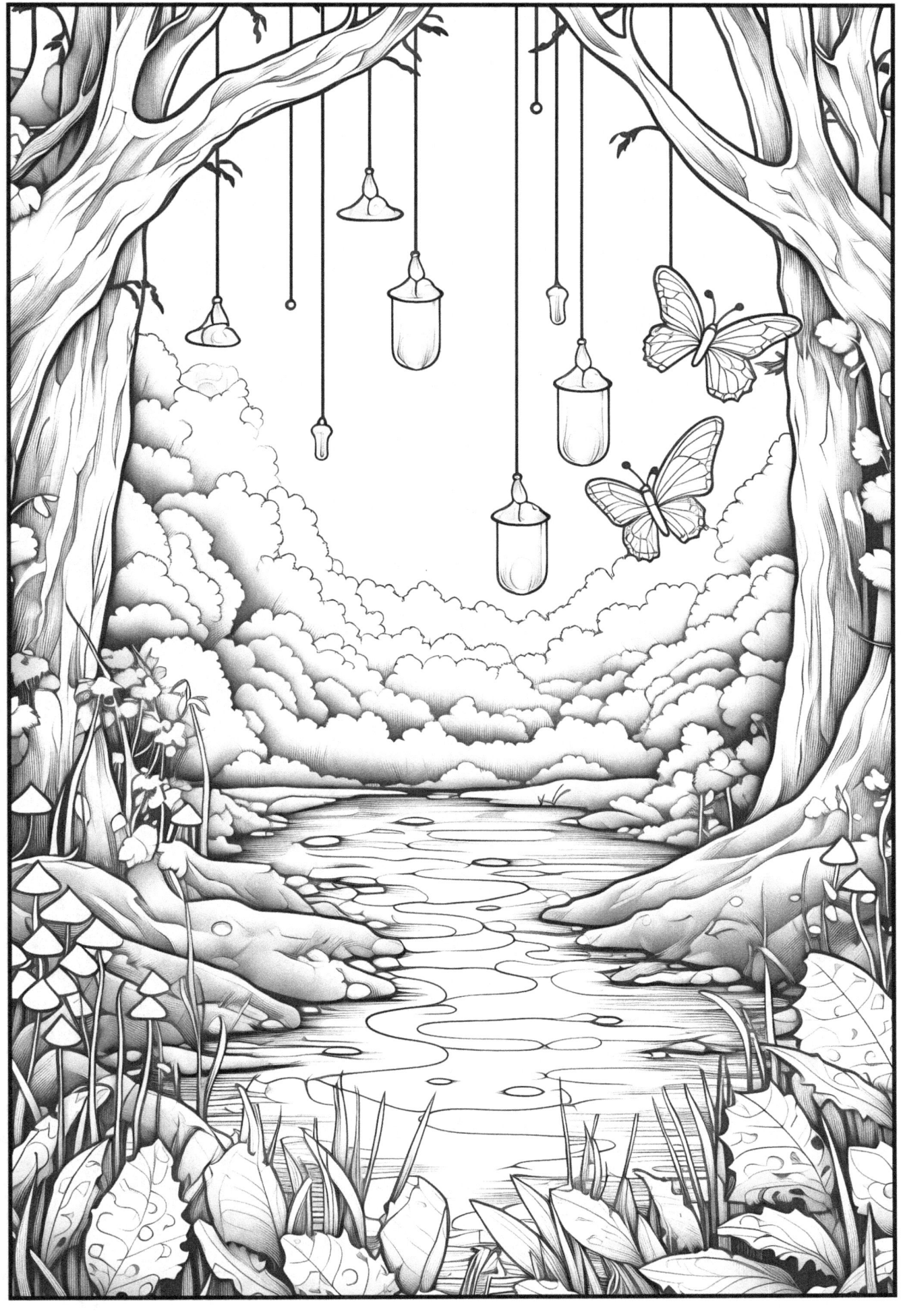

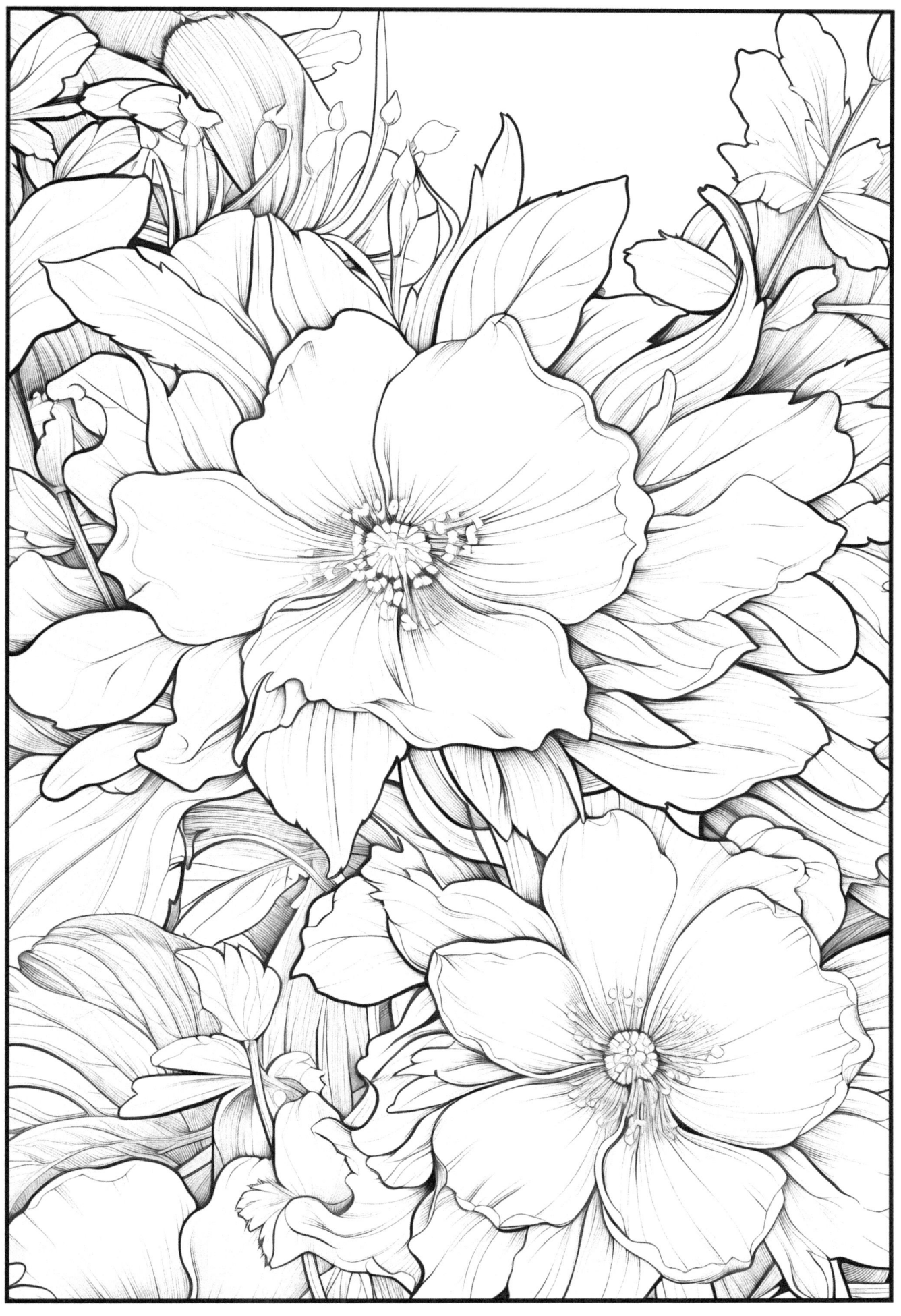